Bernard Miall, Alfred Bertrand

The kingdom of the Barotsi, Upper Zambezia

A Voyage of Exploration in Africa

Bernard Miall, Alfred Bertrand

The kingdom of the Barotsi, Upper Zambezia
A Voyage of Exploration in Africa

ISBN/EAN: 9783337116859

Printed in Europe, USA, Canada, Australia, Japan

Cover: Foto ©ninafisch / pixelio.de

More available books at **www.hansebooks.com**

THE KINGDOM OF THE BAROTSI
Upper Zambezia

A VOYAGE OF EXPLORATION IN AFRICA, RETURNING BY THE VICTORIA FALLS, MATABELELAND, THE TRANSVAAL, NATAL, AND THE CAPE

BY

Alfred Bertrand

Member of the Geographical Society of Geneva
Member of the Royal Geographical Society of London
Member of the Geographical Society of Paris

Translated by A. B. Miall

WITH 47 ILLUSTRATIONS AND TWO MAPS

J. C. JUTA & CO
CAPE TOWN, JOHANNESBURG,
PORT ELIZABETH, STELLENBOSCH

1899

(All rights reserved)

À MES COMPATRIOTES

MM. LES MEMBRES DE LA SOCIÉTÉ DE GÉOGRAPHIE DE
GENÈVE.

TRANSLATOR'S PREFACE

NEWS in a book is no news. At the time of going to press one hears, every day, half a dozen totally divergent accounts of Mr. Rhodes' latest movements, and of the prospects of the Trans-African Railway. All that is certain is that such a railway may be completed, and will be commenced. This indefinite knowledge, however, is sufficient to give the kingdom of the Barotsi an importance and an interest in the eyes of all Englishmen, a significance in which, at the time of Captain Bertrand's exploration, it was somewhat lacking. It may be as well to say a few words as to its present and possible future value.

By the Anglo-Portuguese Treaty of 1891 it was decided that Borotsi should remain within the British sphere of influence. Eight years afterwards, in June of last year, Lewanika accepted the over-lordship of the British South Africa Company.

Immediately after this transfer came the reconquest of the Sudan. Thus the British protectorate in the north, and the British protectorates in the south, are now separated by only some 10° of latitude—by the 400 miles of Lake Tanganyika, bounded by the Congo Free State and German East Africa, and 160 miles of the frontier of these two possessions. In the light of the latest news, this path from Rhodesia to Uganda may soon be open.

This right of way makes possible that gigantic enterprise the Alexandria and Cape Town Railway; it does not necessarily ensure its success. The utility of such an undertaking must largely depend upon a less popular but more significant enterprise—that initiated by Mr. Chamberlain.

We may hope very much from the projected School of Tropical Diseases. We suspect or know to-day that all the most fatal diseases affecting man and beast in tropical countries are communicated by insect-borne, water-borne, air-borne, and other disease-germs. Examination of such media may lead to the determination of the bacillus communicated, and the culture of such bacilli may lead to discoveries which shall make possible the extermination of malaria and the tsetse plague throughout Africa, just as we have stamped out small-pox in England, just as rinderpest is now being eradicated in Africa, thanks to Dr. Koch's production of its antitoxic serum.

Malaria, blackwater fever, enteric fever, yellow fever, beri-beri, tetanus, dysentery, sunstroke, elephantiasis, leprosy—all considered nowadays as parasitic diseases—these are some of the foes that the white man has to encounter in tropical climates. No number of treaties with native chiefs will give us Africa, but one of the greatest wars ever waged, which will be carried on silently in laboratories the public has hardly heard of, by men whose names it does not know. Those who support and those who further this enterprise will not only save life and alleviate suffering; they will be the veritable conquerors of a new world. For to make half the earth habitable to white colonists is as great a thing as to discover a new hemisphere.

Medical science will be followed by engineering and sanitary science. Doubtless much in the way of dam-building, well-sinking, drainage, and irrigation will eventually be found possible even in the worst parts of

Africa, for it is probable that not the least result of the great irrigation dam at Assouan, and the renovation of the Cairo barrage, will be to turn the attention of men and governments, all the world over, to the utilisation of river waters that have been running to waste ever since their first beginnings. Such superficial changes as may be thus effected, together with the clearing of forests in some parts and the planting of trees in others, may go far to ameliorate the extreme differences of temperature and the compression of the rainy season. In short, it is not unreasonable to hope that the advance of civilisation in Africa may make the greater portion of the continent as habitable to the Caucasian as Australia, which is fully as hot, or hotter.

This is a dream of decades, perhaps of generations. But already we can reasonably anticipate the time when tropical Africa will be occupied not only by a few fever-stricken traders and intrepid missionaries, but by actual colonists. When that time comes, the kingdom of the Barotsi, with its great river system, its huge arable tracts, its wealth of timber and iron, and its agricultural population, who are possessed not only with remarkable skill in handicrafts, but with a positive passion for their exercise, must become of immense importance as a cereal-producing and stock-raising and perhaps a manufacturing country. In the near future, according to the prospectors of Rhodesia, we may look forward to an occupation of the country at the invitation of that greatest of all colonisers —mineral wealth. For these reasons Barotsi, a country as large as Germany, is a very significant addition to the Empire, and for the same reasons Captain Bertrand's journal should be of value to every Englishman interested, one way or the other, in the expansion of the Empire—and who is indifferent?

Captain Bertrand deserves our thanks also for showing

us what immense influence a mere handful of missionaries can exert over a savage kingdom, for by this we are able to form some opinion of the far-reaching effects that will follow the progress of the Empire as the missionary of civilisation.

Captain Bertrand's book being a journal, and written largely in the present historical tense, which is seldom pleasing to English ears, I have substituted the preterite throughout the greater part of the volume, preserving the present tense in certain narrative passages. Again, it being a journal, I have also preserved the natural laconism of the original.

I take this opportunity of thanking the friend who, at the author's request, has revised this translation in his absence in South Africa, and who, besides making certain omissions, alterations, and notes, is responsible for the spelling of the native names throughout the book, and has kindly supplied me with material for the third Appendix.

CONTENTS

CHAPTER I.

THE VOYAGE: FROM SOUTHAMPTON TO THE CAPE BY THE "NORHAM CASTLE" 1

CHAPTER II.

IN THE DIAMOND-MINING COUNTRY . 11

From the Cape, *viâ* Kimberley, to Mafeking.

CHAPTER III.

THE HOME OF THE BECHUANAS . 19

From Mafeking to Palapye (capital of Khama, King of the Bamangwato) through Kanye (tribe of Ba-ngwaketsi), Molepololi (tribe of Bakuenas), and the "Thirst Track," near the desert Kalahari.

CHAPTER IV.

IN THE DESERT 41

Across Khama's country—The Great Salt Lake of Makarikari—The Land of the Thousand Vleys.

CHAPTER V.

THE ZAMBEZI 63

On the banks of the River—Kazungula, in Borotsi.

CHAPTER VI.

IN THE KINGDOM OF THE BAROTSI—THE RIVER MACHILI . . 68

To Kazungula—We follow the course of the Machili—We reach the source of the Machili, in the territory of the Mankoya tribe.

CHAPTER VII.

ACROSS THE KINGDOM OF THE BAROTSI 101

Across the Kingdom of the Barotsi to Lealuyi—The Njoko river, in the Matotela country—The Lumbi river—The Lui river, in the Mokwenga country—Sefula.

CHAPTER VIII.

KING LEWANIKA AND THE MISSIONARY, M. COILLARD . . . 134

At Lealuyi, the capital of King Lewanika—Nalolo, the residence of the Mokwai.

CHAPTER IX.

BY CANOE 159

Descending the Zambezi—The region of the rapids—Sesheke.

CHAPTER X.

THE GREAT CATARACTS . 186

Return to Kazungula and Visit to the Victoria Falls.

CHAPTER XI.

IN DISTRESS . . . 198

From the Victoria Falls to Panda-Matenga—The Great "Thirst Trail"—The Gway river (frontier of Matabeleland) and Bulawayo.

CONTENTS

CHAPTER XII.

	PAGE
THE OUTPOSTS OF CIVILISATION	208

Bulawayo, the chief town of Matabeleland.

CHAPTER XIII.

THE GOLD-MINING COUNTRY	218

From Bulawayo, by Matabeleland, to the Transvaal—Pretoria—Johannesburg—The Jameson Raid.

CHAPTER XIV.

THE GARDEN OF SOUTH AFRICA—THE RETURN	244

From Johannesburg to Durban—East London—Port Elizabeth—The Cape—Return to Europe.

APPENDIX I.	271
APPENDIX II.	289
APPENDIX III.	302

MAP I.—THE KINGDOM OF THE BAROTSI.

MAP II.—THE AUTHOR'S ROUTE.

LIST OF ILLUSTRATIONS

PORTRAIT OF THE AUTHOR	*Frontispiece*
	PAGE
CAPE TOWN AND TABLE MOUNTAIN—STORM EFFECT	7
From a photograph	
AVENUE AT WYNBERG	9
From a photograph	
MINERS AT PLAY IN THE COMPOUND	13
From a photograph	
AT MAFEKING, OUR STARTING-POINT	17
Drawn by Baudier, from a photograph by the Author	
THE END OF A TREK	21
From a photograph by the Author	
WE ARRIVE AT KANYE	23
Drawn by Baudier, from a photograph by the Author	
THE PRINCESSES OF KANYE	25
From a photograph by the Author	
OUR WAGGONS	27
From a photograph	
AFRICAN BUSTARD	32
Sketch by Van Hayden. Specimen brought home by the Author	
KING KHAMA	35
From a photograph by the Author	
WOMEN BUILDING HUTS AT PALAPYE	37
From a photograph	

LIST OF ILLUSTRATIONS

	PAGE
THE EXPEDITION EN ROUTE	39
Drawn by Van Muyden	
BLUE GNU	45
Sketch by Van Muyden. Specimen brought home by Author	
WE ADVANCE PAINFULLY	47
Drawn by Boudier, from a photograph by the Author	
HUNTING GNUS	51
Drawn by Van Muyden	
WE ENCAMP UNDER AN "ACACIA GIRAFFA"	53
Drawn by Boudier, from a photograph by the Author	
IN THE BUSH	55
From a photograph by the Author	
A BAOBAB	57
From a photograph by the Author	
DUIKER, "CEPHALOPHUS MERGENS"	60
Sketch by Van Muyden. Specimen brought home by Author	
A DINNER	61
Drawn by Thiriat, from a photograph	
THE ZAMBEZI NEAR ITS CONFLUENCE WITH THE LINYANTI	65
Drawn by Boudier, from a photograph by the Author	
THE MISSIONARY STATION OF M. AND MME LOUIS JALLA	69
Drawn by Boudier, from a photograph by the Author	
LEAVING SCHOOL AT KAZUNGULA	71
From a photograph by the Author	
PRINCE LITIA LEAVING THE CHAPEL	73
From a photograph by the Author	
REEDBUCK, "CERVICAPRA ARUNDINACEA"	77
Sketch by Van Muyden. Specimen brought home by the Author	
LIVINGSTONE'S ELAND, "OREAS CANNA"	78
Sketch by Van Muyden. Specimen brought home by the Author	
HERD OF ZEBRA NEAR THE MACHILI	81
Drawn by Van Muyden	
SNAKE KILLED ON THE MACHILI	82
Sketch by Van Muyden. Specimen brought home by the Author	
CAMP NEAR THE MACHILI	83
From a photograph by the Author	

LIST OF ILLUSTRATIONS

	PAGE
THE LIONESS IS BROUGHT INTO CAMP	85
Drawn by Van Muyden	
MATOTELA SMITHS	89
From a photograph by the Author	
MATOTELA VILLAGE AND GRANARIES	91
Drawn by d'Ouleray, from a photograph by the Author	
NATIVE POCKET-HANDKERCHIEFS	92
Sketch by Van Muyden. Author's collection	
BOW AND POISONED ARROWS: MANKOYA	93
Sketch by Van Muyden. Author's collection	
KOODOO, "STREPSICEROS KUDU"	94
Sketch by Van Muyden. Specimen brought home by Author	
WATERBUCK, "COBUS ELLIPSIPRYMNUS"	95
Sketch by Van Muyden. Specimen brought home by Author	
REID TAKING AN OBSERVATION	99
Drawn by Van Muyden	
COMB OF CARVED WOOD FROM THE BANKS OF THE NJOKO	102
Sketch by Van Muyden. Author's collection	
PILLOW OF CARVED WOOD FROM THE BANKS OF THE NJOKO	103
Sketch by Van Muyden. Author's collection	
A WAR SPEAR, A HUNTING SPEAR, AND A FISH SPEAR	104
Sketch by Van Muyden. Author's collection	
A MATOTELA TYPE	105
From a photograph by the Author	
HUT OF THE CHIEF SIBOUPA	107
Drawn by J. Lavée, from a photograph by the Author	
NATIVES FORDING THE NJOKO	109
Drawn by Boudier, from a photograph by the Author	
THE CHIEF SURUKURUKURU	110
From a photograph by the Author	
"BLUE WATER," THE SUPPOSED SOURCE OF THE IKWE	113
Drawn by Boudier, from a photograph by the Author	
SIBETTE	114
From a photograph by the Author	
CROSSING THE NJOKO	115
From a photograph by the Author	

LIST OF ILLUSTRATIONS

	PAGE
MABONA AND THE MOHOLUHOLU TREE	119
From a photograph by the Author	
MARKET AT MAYUMBA	121
From a photograph by the Author	
CROSSING THE MARSH	123
Drawn by Van Muyden	
DRINKING CALABASH AND SPOONS	124
Sketch by Van Muyden. Author's collection	
HALT!	125
From a photograph by the Author	
A LANDSCAPE IN BOROTSI	127
Drawn by Boudier, from a photograph by the Author	
MY MEN IN THE GREAT BOROTSI PLAIN	129
Drawn by Boudier, from a photograph by the Author	
THE CHURCH AT LEALUYI	131
From a photograph by the Author	
M. COILLARD	135
From a photograph by M. Boissonnas, taken in Geneva	
A ROYAL DISH IN CARVED WOOD, GIVEN BY KING LEWANIKA	137
Sketch by Van Muyden. Author's collection	
STOOL IN CARVED WOOD, GIVEN BY KING LEWANIKA	138
Sketch by Van Muyden. Author's collection	
A HUT OF THE ROYAL HAREM	141
From a photograph by the Author	
WOODEN TUBANA, GIVEN BY KING LEWANIKA	142
Sketch by Van Muyden. Author's collection	
ONE OF LEWANIKA'S COUNCILLORS	145
From a photograph by the Author	
M. AND MME BÉGUIN'S SCHOOL AT NALOLO	149
From a photograph by the Author	
WOODEN FISH-PLATE, GIVEN BY KING LEWANIKA	152
Sketch by Van Muyden. Author's collection	
AT LEALUYI—MME JALLA AND SOME OF HER PUPILS	153
From a photograph by the Author	
AN AXE, GIVEN BY KING LEWANIKA	155
Sketch by Van Muyden. Author's collection	

LIST OF ILLUSTRATIONS

	PAGE
SERIMBA, AND OTHER ROYAL MUSICAL INSTRUMENTS	157
From a photograph by the Author	
I MEET CAPTAIN GIBBONS	163
From a photograph by the Author	
DESCENDING THE ZAMBEZI	165
Drawn by Van Muyden	
THE PORTAGE	169
From a photograph by the Author	
THE KALI RAPIDS	173
Drawn by J. Lavée, from a photograph by the Author	
HUNTING BUFFALO	175
Drawn by Van Muyden	
NEAR LUSHU: THE DEATH RAPIDS	177
From a photograph by the Author	
THE CROCODILE	179
From a photograph by the Author	
THE CANOES ARE STOPPED BY HIPPOPOTAMI	181
Drawn by Van Muyden	
TERRA-COTTA CUP OF THE CHIEF BUMWAI, LEWANIKA'S NEPHEW	187
Sketch by Van Muyden. Author's collection	
THE ELEPHANT TUSK OF 75 LBS.	189
From a photograph by the Author	
NEAR THE VICTORIA FALLS	193
From a photograph by the Author	
PART OF THE VICTORIA FALLS	195
Drawn by G. Vuillier, from a photograph by the Author	
IN DISTRESS! WE ABANDON THE LARGE WAGGON	203
Drawn by Van Muyden	
AT BULAWAYO	209
From a photograph by the Author	
ZULU WARRIORS	213
From a photograph	
NATIVES MAKING FIRE	217
From a photograph	
THE COACH	219
Drawn by Van Muyden	

LIST OF ILLUSTRATIONS

	PAGE
A ZULU WARRIOR	221
From a photograph	
PRETORIA GOVERNMENT HOUSE	225
From a photograph	
JOHANNESBURG MARKET	229
From a photograph	
PRESIDENT KRÜGER'S RESIDENCE AT PRETORIA	241
From a photograph	
VIEW OF DURBAN	245
From a photograph	
A PLANTER'S HOUSE	247
From a photograph	
HINDOO COOLIES PICKING TEA	249
Drawn by Bowdier, from a photograph	
THE MERINDOL RIVER, NATAL	251
From a photograph	
A SHAM FIGHT	253
From a photograph	
A PRETTY CORNER, NEAR KEARSNEY, NATAL	255
From a photograph	
DURBAN "RICKSHAWS"	257
From a photograph	
EAST LONDON FROM THE SEA	259
From a photograph	
HOW ONE LANDS AT EAST LONDON AND PORT ELIZABETH	261
From a photograph	
THE QUAYS, CAPE TOWN	265
Drawn by Taylor, from a photograph	

THE KINGDOM OF THE BAROTSI

CHAPTER I

THE VOYAGE: FROM SOUTHAMPTON TO THE CAPE BY THE "NORHAM CASTLE."

AFTER having visited various parts of the world, I felt for a long time a keen desire to explore some portion of the mysterious continent of Africa. This project took shape when Mr. Percy C. Reid (ex-officer of the 15th Hussars and nephew to Sir Henry Barkly, sometime Governor of the Cape), with whom I made a journey into Kashmir and the Himalaya some years ago, proposed that I should join an expedition which was then being formed with the object of penetrating the kingdom of the Barotsi, in Upper Zambezia, on the threshold of Central Africa, and of surveying a part of that country. The expedition was organised by Captain A. St. Hill Gibbons, of the 3rd Yorkshire Regiment; Mr. F. D. Pirie, a Scotsman, completed our staff.

Captain Gibbons and Pirie have preceded us by several weeks to Africa, in order to buy oxen, horses, waggons, &c., and to engage the necessary men. We shall rejoin them at Mafeking, in the western part of the Transvaal.

Mafeking, which is eight hundred miles from the Cape, is at present the terminus of the railway, and thither Reid and I shall set out immediately upon disembarking, and thence our expedition will start.

To reach the Borotsi country we shall follow approximately the following route: through Molepololi and Palapye to Bechuanaland, and thence, leaving the desert of Kalahari on the west, we shall skirt the eastern borders of the great salt lake of Makarikari in order to cross the " Land of the Thousand Vleys " at its northern extremity.

We hope to cross the Zambezi in the beginning of July, at its junction with the Chobe or Linyanti, and shall then speedily find ourselves in a virgin country. So much being said, I take up my journal :—

March 23, 1895.—We embark at Southampton, on board the *Norham Castle* (Castle Line). Soon after leaving the Solent we come across a rough sea: the Bay of Biscay of evil repute.

March 26*th*. — Seas tumultuous; we have had two squalls of great violence. According to one of the officers on board, the *Norham Castle* may consider herself lucky in not having had to encounter many others.

March 27*th*.—The waves are calming: splendid sun. We have been delayed by the gale, and are trying to make up for lost time. The passengers, many of whom have been invisible since the beginning of the voyage, are one by one emerging from their cabins; more or less pallid, but on the whole sea-sickness is vanishing. This is the time for making acquaintances. There are forty-two saloon passengers on the register; men of business, engineers, and so forth, returning to their posts, and several officers rejoining their regiments.

March 28th.—This morning we passed the naked coast of the island of Porto Santo. The contrast to Madeira, which we were not long in sighting, was a striking one. We steamed along the eastern coast: the slopes of the mountains, of a beautiful green, stood out with remarkable intensity from the blue surrounding us on all sides.

Having doubled Cape Garajao, we entered the pretty bay above which Funchal, the capital of Madeira, rises in graceful stages. Scarcely was the anchor down but we were surrounded by a swarm of canoes, some paddled by native boys, who dive after the smallest coins thrown to them, others by sellers of oranges, bananas, or custard apples. Some of these, wishing to hasten the sale of their products, conceived the unhappy idea of scrambling along the nettings of the main-rails without permission; they were received a little rudely by sailors posted at the points of invasion and armed with rope's-ends. They must have been accustomed to this kind of reception, and did not lose their tempers: not even one who, in his haste to return to his canoe, took an unpremeditated bath, to the great delight of his comrades.

The steamer waited here for several hours to coal and re-victual. We took the opportunity to go ashore, and made the ascent to the church of Nossa Senhora Monte by the new railway: an enchanting journey. The line winds through the midst of gardens planted with sugar-cane and bananas. Here were camellias in flower: further, some children threw roses at us. From the terrace of the church, embowered in foliage, we were able to admire the bay stretched out at our feet. On the tranquil waters we distinguished the *Norham Castle*, which seemed asleep: truly the image of "le port après la tempête."

We made the descent in one of those osier baskets called "carro"; rapid conveyances, thanks to the sloping roads paved with shining cobble-stones. Two islanders, cord in hand, run on either side of the "carro" and maintain equilibrium; the speed attained is considerable. We still had time to visit the fruit market, and to gather flowers in the garden of Mill's Hotel, a veritable little Eden with its hot-house vegetation. The clouds prevented our seeing the Corral, one of the highest mountains in the island, whose summit I climbed some years ago.

The vineyards of Madeira, lately destroyed by phylloxera, are in great measure rehabilitated. Funchal is growing; it numbers at present 30,000 souls out of a total population of 140,000 for the whole island. We re-embarked just before sailing.

March 29th.—Fine weather. From an early hour we had in sight the peak of Teneriffe (12,000 feet), which dominates the island, the most important in the Canaries. The base was concealed; we saw only the snow-clad peak emerging from the morning mists. In the course of the afternoon we cast anchor for a short time in order to disembark two or three passengers at a distance of some hundreds of yards from Santiago de Santa Cruz. We were not allowed to land, so we enjoyed the picturesque landscape before us from the deck. At a distance these white, rose, and brown houses, embowered in foliage, have a most charming effect.

While we were in the roads, the *Norham Castle* was attended, as at Madeira, by numbers of canoes, whose possessors sought to induce the passengers to buy tobacco and cigars, which were pronounced excellent. Although their merchandise is different, these Spaniards make as much noise and as many demonstrations as their Portuguese neighbours of Madeira.

Teneriffe has 95,000 inhabitants; its capital, Santiago de Santa Cruz, contains 20,000.

After Teneriffe we shall not see land again until we reach the Cape.

March 30th.—We crossed the tropic of Cancer, and five days later the equator. On entering the austral hemisphere we say *au revoir* to the Pole Star, which disappears below our horizon; our point of reckoning will henceforth be the Southern Cross. Our activity is now, by force of circumstances, entirely concentrated upon the life on board. Besides the time consecrated to work and reading, this life offers plenty of interest to one who has eyes to see and ears to hear. The passengers make themselves acquainted with the various kinds of work performed on a steamer like ours—one of 4,500 tons, lit by electricity to its furthest recesses. The discipline is admirable at every degree of the hierarchic scale. Others can acquire notions of astronomy, or learn to handle the sextant. But all delight in the spectacle offered by the ocean in all its many phases, and in the tropical sunsets, whose magnificence, as well as that of the starry nights, defies all description. And unexpected sights are not wanting; one day whales are seen in the offing; schools of dolphin come to play on the surface of the water; flying fish leap from wave to wave, and sea-birds also visit us from time to time.

In the evenings eight musicians, forming part of the crew, make the air ring with their lively echoes, in addition to which several " musical evenings " have been organised by amateurs, without counting games of all kinds, and interesting conversations.

Finally, despite the heat, two half-days have been given up to the athletic sports which the English never abandon under any pretext, nor in any latitude. Excellent principle: for this practice not only develops the body and keeps it in good health, but is also a discipline for the character, and produces courage, perseverance, and endurance.

On Sunday, worship in the large after-saloon. The Bible is placed on the national flag. If we had no clergyman passenger on board, the religious service, following the usage of the English navy, would be celebrated by the captain.

While I am speaking of the staff of the *Norham Castle*, I cannot help mentioning, as an example of the courage of these sailors, the conduct of the first officer, Mr. Frank Whitehead, who, for the intrepid courage and devotion that he displayed on the 7th of April last, has been the object recently in England of the most flattering and deserved distinctions, and has received Lloyd's silver medal, the silver medal of the Federation of Shipping Agents of Great Britain, and a testimonial from the "Liverpool Shipwreck and Humane Society." The *Norham Castle*, while passing the inhospitable coast of Natal, found herself at daybreak in sight of a four-masted vessel stranded on a reef. The shipwrecked sailors made signals of distress from the rigging. Captain Duncan found that his steamer could not approach the reef; so he immediately lowered two life-boats, of which one was commanded by Whitehead, who judged that it would be folly to attempt to board the wreck. He accordingly had a line tied round his body, and plunged into the waves, one of the ship-wrecked sailors doing the same. The two strong swimmers met and fastened their lines together, by which means seventeen lives were saved. The captain of the four-master, who would not quit his ship until all his men were safe and sound, was himself so seriously hurt that he could be saved only by a different means.

Once more Whitehead plunged into the sea, and, after an heroic struggle, succeeded in rescuing the captain alive.

We hope to reach the Cape on Friday, April 11th. From Southampton we shall have accomplished some six thousand miles in nineteen days—about one quarter of the earth's circumference. In this short space of time we have passed through winter on leaving Europe, spring at Madeira, summer under the tropics, and autumn at the Cape.

April 11th.—The presence of numbers of birds foretells a speedy arrival; cormorants, black as jet, migrating to the south.

Land! Here is Cape Town, so well situated on the shores of the bay. It lies at the foot of Table Mountain, whose sides are precipitous, and whose summit, seen from the sea, appears flat. It is flanked by two other summits—the Lion's Head and the Devil's Peak.

In the distance other mountains form a picturesque sight, blurred by fog and bounding the horizon.

It is a strange sensation, that of finding one's self on *terra firma* after a long voyage. The body, accustomed to rolling and pitching, still sways to and fro for a time.

We are surrounded by a multi-coloured crowd; every shade of white and black is represented.

The first impression received at Cape Town is that of a city whose plan is well conceived, but whose outskirts perhaps leave something to be desired. The streets in general intersect at a right angle, and are bordered by houses with flat roofs.

April 12th.—Day of rest. We cannot get our baggage from the custom-house. This afternoon a carriage drive of several miles through the environs of Wynberg, a veritable park intersected by avenues of remarkable beauty, planted with oak, eucalyptus, Scotch firs, &c., with glimpses

AVENUE AT WYNBERG
From a photograph

of the sea and mountains. Numerous country houses, surrounded by flower gardens, stand out from the background of foliage. We admired a shrub with silver foliage, justly called the "silver tree." These plantations of forest trees, so beautifully situated, are due to the foresight of the first Dutch colonists.

April 13th.—It is raining; a rain much desired by the inhabitants. We must remember that here in the Cape we are at the end of autumn; winter is at the door.

Reid set out yesterday for Johannesburg. We have made arrangements to meet next Wednesday at Mafeking in Bechuanaland, to the west of the Transvaal. I shall take train this evening, and in thirty-six hours expect to be in Kimberley, the "diamond-town," on the frontier of Griqueland and the Orange Free State, where I shall stop for a day and a half.

Thanks to the kindness of Captain W———, who is about to occupy an important situation in the British South African Company, I have obtained a permit to visit throughout one of the most famous diamond mines of the world, the "De Beers Consolidated Mines, Limited." Going down Adderley Street, the principal thoroughfare, before our departure, we admired the fine avenues, another legacy of the Dutch rule. We passed the sumptuous Parliament House, the Governor's house (which is very simple), and went into the Botanic Gardens, where we saw a great variety of trees and plants, exotic and indigenous.

Let me say in passing that although Cape Town has been in existence for about two hundred years, it has rather the look of a modern city. With its suburbs, it contains at present 85,000 inhabitants, white and coloured, representatives of almost every race of Southern Africa, besides a fair number of Malays. Its commerce is considerable.

CHAPTER II

IN THE DIAMOND-MINING COUNTRY

From the Cape, *via* Kimberley, to Mafeking.

HERE we are on April 14th, *en route* since yesterday night. According to what I have read, we travelled last night over one of the most beautiful parts of the railway; remarkable mountains, districts producing wine, cereals, horses, sheep, cattle, and ostriches—in short, a very rich country.

This morning we awoke at Matjesfontein, at the entrance of the Great Karroo tableland, which we shall skirt all day and all night, arriving at Kimberley to-morrow.

This plain, despite its aridity, is marked by oases here and there, and is not wanting in a certain grandeur.

April 15th.—I presented myself at the office of the "De Beers Consolidated Mines, Limited," this morning, my letter of introduction in my pocket. The secretary, Mr. W. H. C——, gave me a card of permission to visit this celebrated diamond mine in detail.

Let us recollect that in the month of March, 1888, Mr. Cecil John Rhodes was the creator of the powerful company known as the "De Beers Consolidated Mines, Limited." Besides the De Beers mines, it comprises those of Kimberley, Dutoitspan, and Bulfontein, and to-day holds the diamond market in its power.

The following account is partly drawn from the interesting reports which have been courteously sent me. I shall be brief in the narration of this visit.

According to the survey of the mining engineers, it has been conjectured that these mines were formed by anciently extinct volcanoes, which became filled with volcanic mud by inferior pressure. The diamondiferous earth, called "blue ground," is accordingly found in a kind of funnel.

According to the latest report we have seen, there are more than 1,500 whites at work in these mines, without counting the superior employés, and 6,600 blacks.

Our guide conducted us in the first place to the "compound," an enclosed space covering several acres. In order to prevent the theft of diamonds, the black workers are obliged to confine themselves to this enclosure when they are not at work in the mine. They work eight hours out of the twenty-four, and in general sign a four months' contract.

Buildings of corrugated iron, each containing twenty blacks, are placed round the side of this immense square courtyard, which is enclosed by iron palings. There are stores which sell provisions of the highest quality at very low prices, but no alcoholic drinks; there is also a swimming-bath, and an admirably appointed hospital. Missionaries hold classes in the compound.

Kaffirs, Basutos, Zulus, Bechuanas, Matabele, Makalaka, &c., more or less well draped in multi-coloured garments, cook their food, wash their clothes, chop their firewood (which is furnished gratuitously by the Company), smoke, and chatter among themselves. It is a picture not wanting in local colour.

On arriving at one of the shafts of the mine we changed our clothes for more appropriate costumes, and rapidly descended into the bowels of the earth. We stopped at the last gallery (1,200 feet), which is cut in

MISERS AT PLAY IN THE COMPOUND
From a photograph

the solid rock, to reach the funnel containing the diamondiferous earth. We then visited the two parallel galleries, 960 feet and 1,000 feet below the surface, whence the earth has been mined for a long time. Great activity reigns in these galleries, which are lit by electricity. The earth is removed in little waggons running on rails to a part whence it is sent to the surface by a powerful engine which pumps out water at the same time.

Once more we breathed the fresh air, and after a good bath a very necessary thing—we continued our inspection.

When the blue diamond-bearing earth has been brought up from the mine it is exposed to the open air; the action of the atmosphere sooner or later renders it friable. Recently the Company has been obliged to erect a battery of crushing machines, for part of the earth brought up remains impervious to the action of sun and air. These machines can crush as many as 1500 tons in ten hours. The portable engine which runs them is of 1100 horse-power.

Next we watched the washing-machine at its work, in which the diamond-bearing is separated from the ordinary earth; then comes the turn of another machine, the "pulsator," which performs a second and more minute sifting.

After these operations what remains of the diamond-bearing earth passes through the hands of the sorters properly so called. We entered a hall where we saw a number of employés who are subjected to supervision at every moment. Here they sort diamonds to the value of £10,000 daily.

Every day, when the sorting is over, the diamonds are sent under armed escort to the principal office, there to be delivered over to experts.

We finish this interesting day by sleeping at Kenilworth, a model village built by the De Beers Company for their white employés. This village is truly worthy of admiration.

April 16th. — This morning permission was kindly accorded us to visit the principal office of the company, where we were enabled to follow the different processes through which the diamonds must pass before arriving at the perfected state. To clean them, they are boiled in a mixture of nitric and sulphuric acids; they are then sorted according to their size, purity, and colour.

The colour of diamonds is variable; it may be clear white, opaque white, green, pink, blue, yellow, brown, or orange. The size varies from the dimensions of a pin's head to that of the largest diamond ever found, whose weight uncut was $428\frac{1}{2}$ carats. After the first cutting it still weighed $228\frac{1}{2}$ carats. It figured in the Exposition Universelle de Paris of 1889.

The little cup of diamonds put before our eyes and sorted in our presence was worth £60,000. A single one of these diamonds, which was handed us for examination, was valued at over £600; its colour was a fine yellow.

The last operation consists of resorting diamonds into lots, which are examined by experts. These lots are sold to agents living in the neighbourhood, who represent the principal European diamond merchants.

The city of Antwerp has almost the monopoly of cutting the Cape diamonds.

Kimberley, a town of 15,000 to 20,000 inhabitants, contains all the necessaries of life. P——, one of the pioneers of this country, tells me that when he arrived in 1870 there was not a single house built on the site of the present city.

At midday we take our places in the train and in eighteen hours arrive at Mafeking, the terminus of the line; a grass country where many herds and flocks of sheep and cattle graze and grow fat.

During the journey we crossed the river Hart, a tributary of the Orange River, and entered Bechuanaland.

We are now leaving civilisation behind; the clustering huts of native villages become more and more frequent; the railway stations are mere shanties of galvanized iron, and the passengers who came on board are more and more picturesque of aspect.

April 21st.—Mafeking, with the neighbouring farms, possesses 2,000 to 3,000 inhabitants. It is the starting-place of all caravans for the interior. It has a distinct individuality, caused both by the inhabitants and the place itself, which gives the impression of a vast camp, with a constant movement of waggons drawn by long teams of oxen. Among the whites one sees bronzed, energetic faces which show that the struggle for life is not an empty phrase in this country.

At the entrance to Mafeking a number of tents stand out on the veldt, which are inhabited for the moment by 150 mounted troopers, part of the little colonial army of Bechuanaland. Very characteristic this light uniform and the brown felt hat with the white band, rakishly turned up at the side. A troop of picked men, always ready for action; they have attained a remarkable degree of endurance. One of their officers told me that Lieutenant P——, who, during the war against the Matabele last year, had the management of a Maxim gun, received a shot in the right arm. Despite this terrible wound, which made amputation necessary later, he made a journey on horseback, I don't know how many days in length, before he could get it dressed.

How busy we have been! It is hard to recount all the preparations necessary for such an expedition as ours.

We have fourteen horses, or ponies, for saddle only, thirty-four oxen, and seventeen pack-donkeys. Also several dogs; in particular, a superb pair of bull-dogs as watch-dogs.

Also a large four-wheeled waggon, weighing, when loaded, nearly 7,000 lbs., and two two-wheeled waggons (Scotch carts), which carry between them a load of

AT MAFEKING, OUR STARTING-POINT
Drawn by Boudier, from a photograph by the Author

5,000 lbs. One of the latter has already set out under the charge of Captain Gibbons.

The day has been devoted to lading the waggons and arranging the departure; now all is finished, and we are ready to take the field. We start to-morrow.

Despite the fatigue of the journey, Reid, at the request of one of the inhabitants, has taken to-night nine observations with the sextant; five of Sirius O., and four of Arcturus E., in order to determine once more the position of Mafeking.

CHAPTER III

THE HOME OF THE BECHUANAS

From Mafeking to Palapye (capital of Khama, King of the Bamangwato) through Kanye (tribe of Bangwaketsi), Molepololi (tribe of Bakuenas), and the "Thirst Track," near the desert of Kalahari.

ON the 22nd of April we give the last touch to the preparations for departure. The oxen are examined and yoked, the horses and donkeys assembled at the starting-point, our men at their respective posts. For the moment, the staff consists of Adam and Jacobus, drivers of the waggons, who are armed with immense whips (the stock nearly five feet and the lash more than eighteen feet in length) and are responsible for the teams.

They are seconded by two "leaders," Franz and his comrade. One of their principal duties is to go to the head of the first yoke of oxen in difficult passages.

Finally, George and Pony have charge of the horses and donkeys. Pony, when he has time, helps us with cooking and washing clothes.

Our own duties—besides the thousand occupations that these imply—will be to hold ourselves in readiness to put a hand to everything and anything on all occasions.

At three o'clock the signal for departure is given. This is the order of march: the large waggon, with its eight yoke of oxen, forms by itself a column seventy feet long; next the small waggon drawn by four yoke of oxen; next the drove of horses and donkeys, for the moment more or less well disciplined, and also the spare oxen. The dogs gambol right and left along the column.

What follows will prove that, from the very outset, there were not wanting all kinds of difficulties and complications to hinder our keeping the whole assemblage in good order. These complications, difficulties, and annoyances were continually presenting themselves in different guises of which it is certainly difficult to form any idea amid the facilities of civilised life. The great thing is always to go forward, without accepting any check, and to know how to make the best of circumstances. Reid, who has a long experience of Africa, is a great help to us.

At last we are *en route*, going in a northerly direction.

At nightfall the leading waggon gets stuck in crossing a marshy plain. We double the team;—in spite of all our efforts we can't get it out; here perforce, where we have foundered, we must strike our first camp for the night. We have to go and cut firewood in the neighbouring thickets in the darkness, prepare supper, outspan the oxen, tether the horses round the waggons, and give them their rations of maize, &c.

During this march the second leader disappeared, and also one of the spare oxen; we never saw either again.

April 23rd.—Rose at sunrise; we found the oxen grazing already. As yesterday, and on the following days, we had to forage for the horses, cut wood for cooking, and put all in order for departure. Presently, spade in hand, we had to extricate a foundered wheel. The teams being refreshed, after a vigorous effort we set forth again on our journey. We are skirting the western frontier of the Transvaal.

At half-past ten, halt!—the end of the first trek, or march; the beasts are pastured till three o'clock in the afternoon, at which hour we inspan for the second trek,

THE END OF A TREK
From a photograph by the Author.

which takes us to Ramatlaban, the limit of the colony and protectorate of Bechuanaland. The *pièce de résistance* of our evening meal consists of two ducks killed and plucked on the way. The third and last trek of the day occupies us till ten at night.

April 24th.— It was cold enough last night, and there was a heavy dew. We warmed ourselves by pottering about at our various occupations. During the first trek the pole of the leading waggon broke clean in two, just when the waggon was going over an enormous stone—for stones and ruts are the two elements of which the trail we follow is composed. We repaired the damage indifferently enough with a heavy chain. As yesterday, we are traversing a grass country, slightly undulating, studded with mimosas, and giving the impression of an immense park. Here and there pheasants and partridges show themselves; we have also seen steinbock (*Nanotragus tragulus*).

April 25th.—Two horses and two donkeys got away last night. Luckily they were brought back to camp. A hard day—three treks: the last until half-past ten at night. These night marches are favourable to the teams but difficult and harassing for us, for after having encamped a good deal of time elapses before everything is put in order and we can turn in. Moreover, the horses and donkeys linger behind, straying and grazing in the scrub.

April 26th.—Three horses and six donkeys were missing at this morning's muster; George and Pony were sent to look for them. After several hours they rejoined us; two donkeys are definitely lost, also one of the bull-dogs.

In the distance we have in view the woodland hills that we must cross to reach Kanye to-morrow. We are badly shaken by the stony roads, which put the interior of the waggons in disorder.

April 27th.—Arrived in the early morning at Kanye. The round huts of the native village, built of red earth with roofs of thatch, are scattered at the top and bottom of the hill. Great animation; numerous waggons em-

WE ARRIVE AT KANYE.
Drawn by Boudier, from a photograph by the Author

ployed by the merchants of the country. Accompanied by one of the few Europeans resident in Kanye, we climbed up to the dwelling of the chief, Bathoen,[*] to ask his permission to take a couple of his subjects into our service. Unfortunately he is absent for some time. The chief's hut, situated in front of the "assembly place," is different from those of his vassals. It resembles a cottage.

[*] One of the two chiefs who accompanied Khama to England.

and there is a primitive verandah on one side. Here we saluted the princess, who was draped in brilliant colours and wore a red turban. She could not give an answer to our request without her spouse's authority. We entered the chamber of honour, where I discovered on a what-not a Bible translated into the language of the country, for Bathoen is a professing Christian.

At my request the princess consented to be photographed, but she wished to be clad in her finest raiment, so I had to return later. At the appointed hour I found the princess got up in a cream silk dress of European cut and a blue bonnet surmounted by an enormous yellow rose! How I regretted the change from the picturesque costume of an hour before! Her mother-in-law, in blue, and her sister-in-law, in red, wished to make part of the group. Then the Minister of State asked to be photographed; then others; I thought all my plates would have been used!

We visited the new church built by the missionary, the Rev. Mr. Good, near the chief's hut.

All huts belonging to the same family are surrounded by high palisades of branches. Castor-oil plants grow wild.

Great fertility of soil; in one garden we saw excellent vegetables grown from seeds imported from Europe.

Kanye is the capital of the tribe of the Ba-ngwaketsi; the chief Bathoen is independent; the tribe numbers 7,000 or 10,000 persons, who apply themselves to raising stock, and trafficking in grain, skins, &c. We learn here that Captain Gibbons, who preceded us by several days with two saddle horses and a small waggon drawn by eight oxen, has had an accident. His waggon was overturned; he got off with a crushed finger.

In the afternoon we set out again; as we are without guides we camp for the night near the village of

THE PRINCESSES OF KANO.
From a photograph by the Author

Motschuaneng; jackals are baying in the neighbourhood.

April 28th.—Enchanting country; we are passing through the Makarupu mountains. Some stray horses were not recovered until the middle of the day.

Pirie and I, installed in the large waggon, were quietly chatting when we were suddenly thrown to the ground. We got up without a scratch, but we perceived with stupefaction our "Noah's ark" lying on its right side! The driver had not been able to avoid a sudden depression of the earth. There was no room for hesitation; we had to set to work, and, despite a broiling sun, unloaded part of the contents. We had much trouble in raising the enormous vehicle, which happily did not suffer any serious damage in its fall. At least two hours lost!

April 29th.—As yesterday, a beautiful country, mountainous and wooded. This morning, at an early hour, we had a visit from some natives, who brought us curdled milk in a leather bottle. This country is thinly sown with cattle posts, where, in the proper season, the proprietors send their herds under the care of slaves; these slaves remind one of the Russian serfs of the *ancien régime*.

Despite the great abundance of cattle, it is impossible to obtain fresh milk from these people; they consider it unwholesome. All their milk is curdled; this operation is performed by natural means, for, on principle, they never clean the vessels into which they put it.

We met some natives mounted on bullocks; a cord passed through the nostrils served as bridle; they travelled at a fair rate.

A huge cloud of locusts went by to our right; we took them at first sight for a dense smoke. At last we came to within sight of the native village of Mashupa (Gattin),

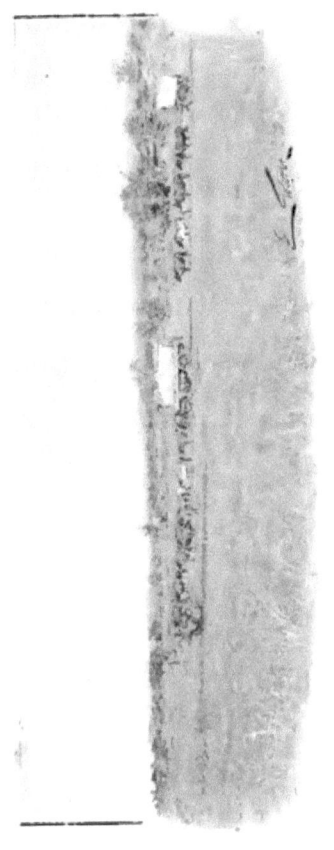

OUR WAGONS
From a photograph

where we were to halt ; we had to cross only one more plain to reach it, and so earn a well-deserved repast. It was almost crossed, when suddenly we were stopped again ; this time in the sand ! The teams were doubled to draw us out of our fix, but to no end. We had to unyoke, turn our beasts to graze, and rest ourselves. Surrounded by numbers of inquisitive natives we lit our fire and prepared breakfast under a burning sky. Then we unloaded the back of the waggon, set it moving once more, loaded up again and set out, not without letting Adam, the driver, hear what he had done! But this did not prevent his getting us stuck in the sand a second time in the evening while crossing a dry watercourse.

April 30th. — Adam ran off during the night, so we have raised Jacobus, with whom we are very well satisfied, to the dignity of driver to the large waggon. Reid, not as a first attempt, took charge of the other waggon, and we set off. We were anxious to make up for lost time, and made without any disaster three treks in the daytime and a good march at night as well. We do not regret Adam, who was not up to his work, and who, as he thought himself quite an indispensable personage, took an intolerable attitude.

May 1st. The country was more open ; we passed through a long valley. At midday we arrived at Molepololi, situated at the top of a hill, the headquarters of the tribe of the Bakuenas (Crocodiles), whose chief is Sebele. This afternoon we had an audience in the council place.

At the moment of our arrival, his Highness, surrounded by a score of his subjects, was seated in a dignified manner on an antelope-skin. After the usual introductions, we asked his permission to take into our service a few of his subjects, foreseeing a favourable reply.

His Highness has not the good reputation of his neighbour of Kanye, but he made no objection to my photographing him and his spouse; he even condescended to be interested in the apparatus, the working of which I explained to him as well as I could.

We shall give men and beasts a breathing-space of forty-eight hours, and shall set out in the morning of the day after to-morrow for Palapye.

Molepololi has about 6,000 inhabitants; the trade is in cereals, stock, and skins of wild beasts.

May 3rd.—We left Molepololi after deciding to follow a trail not generally used, in order to reach Palapye; it is called the "Thirst Track," as it is near the desert of Kalahari, and water is rare there.

Sebele, chief of the tribe of Bakuenas, gave orders to three of his subjects to accompany us as far as Palapye; the direction is north-east. We halted for several hours at Klippan, a village where one of Sebele's brothers, who is in opposition to him, has taken refuge with his partisans. We received the visits of numerous inhabitants, men, women, and children, who watched our every movement. The details of our cookery seemed above all to interest the ladies of the place, whilst their husbands showed a particular predilection for the firearms. The costumes in general are simple enough; they consist of cotton stuffs and skins of wild beasts; as ornaments, bracelets, and anklets, preferably blue. One young girl, whose head had been entirely shaven, with the exception of the crown, had the remnant of her curly fleece smothered with fat.

May 4th.—Since yesterday afternoon we have been passing through a wooded and slightly undulating country. The teams sink deep in the sand, and advance with difficulty; we regret the rich pastures of the preceding days. A stiff march at night up to half-past eleven.

May 5th.—We let the cattle rest, and did not yoke them until late in the day. The nearness of the desert of Kalahari made itself felt, and the oxen were still struggling in the sand.

We have decided to start to-morrow morning at half-past two, and we do what we shall often do in future—organise a watch to rouse man and beast at the desired hour. The watch between one and two is allotted to me: picturesque effect of moonlight in the camp. The tired men sleep near the fire in various postures; the horses doze at their tethers round the waggons; the oxen and asses graze hard by.

May 6th.—Shortly after breakfast Reid killed a small, flat-headed snake with a blow of a stick. In the course of the day Reid and I set out on horseback, reconnoitring for the wells of Botenama, which we knew would not be far away. We met three native hunters, who could only give us vague directions as to the well in question; such is generally the case in this country, where water is precious. We finished by discovering the well, overshadowed by mimosas, and watered the beasts a few at a time; they had been twenty-eight hours without water.

We remained two days at the Botenama well to rehabilitate man and beast. An antelope recently killed was a much appreciated addition to our diet. Great differences of temperature; hot by day and cold by night.

This well, a very ancient one, was repaired by Sebele. It is built of large stones simply piled one on another; it is about six feet in diameter and twenty-five feet deep.

May 9th.—We crossed a charming wooded country,

stocked with pheasants and partridges, which formed the *menu* of our dinner. It is scattered over with enormous conical ant-hills; we measured one ten feet in height. We arrived at the Selynia lake, where we found the water muddy; but we had to content ourselves with it. We found the spoor of three giraffes in the sand.

Next came a wide plain covered with yellowed grasses, where we enjoyed a splendid moonrise, without any twilight. We saw in the distance a long trail of smoke — the veldt on fire.

May 10*th.*— The water was served out in rations; not a drop of the precious liquid was to be lost. At nightfall the horses broke suddenly into full trot; they took us to a lake which the poor beasts, having again been twenty-four hours without water, had foretold by instinct.

One of our dogs, Toby, has a marked predilection for jackals. He has killed three in two nights.

We discovered some time ago that the best geographical charts of this country are no better than sketch-maps; they are full of inaccuracies.

May 11*th.*—A complete change of scene: we are travelling through a mountainous country, wooded and picturesque. Before breakfast we reconnoitred by climbing to the top of a kopje composed of enormous blocks of reddish rocks hidden in verdure, and there discovered other ranges of mountains: the Mangwato Hills. The morning silence was broken only by the call of partridges and the various cries of baboons.

During the day Reid killed a bustard of twenty pounds weight, which at night afforded us an excellent supper at the camp of Ramanena, of happy memory, where we found the water muddy, it is true, but in abundance, and where some shepherds brought us milk and wild honey.

May 12th.—As yesterday, an enchanting woodland country; a refreshing breeze. We cross the bed of the river Mahalapsi, which we use and abuse with delight; it is the best we have come across for a long time. Later on we cross the Milti, at present dry.

May 13th.—We joined Captain Gibbons, about eighteen miles on the hither side of Palapye.

May 14th.—Arrived to-day at Palapye, three weeks after our departure from Mafeking.

AFRICAN BUSTARD
Sketch by Van Maydon. Specimen brought home by the Author

May 17th.—To rest the expedition we have been stopping several days in Palapye, or Palapchwe, the capital of Khama, king of the Bamangwato. We take the opportunity to change some of our men, who, on account of their dialect, would be of no use to us further north. The waggons are repaired, also the stores; we are completely furnished with provisions, and all preparations have been made for going forward.

Palapye (pop. 25,000), the capital of the Bamangwato tribe, is situated in a fertile country at the foot of the Choping Hills. The people trade in skins and cereals.

THE HOME OF THE BECHUANAS 33

Khama, an influential chief, was educated by missionaries, the successors of Robert Moffat and Livingstone, who, as every one knows, preached the gospel for many years in Bechuanaland.

Khama is a Christian, by conviction and in practice. He exerts a powerful and beneficent influence over his people, by whom he is much beloved, and of whom many

KING KHAMA
From a photograph by the Author

have embraced the Christian faith. It is said by all, white and black, that Khama is the wisest and most enlightened chief in Africa. The best proof of this is that he does not allow the introduction of any alcoholic drink into his kingdom.*

* King Khama came to Europe, in the course of the year 1895, to lay this question before Queen Victoria, and to ask for her authority

Khama called on us in our camp on the very morning of our arrival, we returning the call a few hours later.

We found the king at the *lekhothla*, a deliberative assembly which administers justice every morning, meeting in a large courtyard, some hundreds of yards in circumference, enclosed by rough palings.

Khama, surrounded by some thirty of his subjects, came forward to meet us. He made us sit down in the shade of a tree, and then, with the usual forms, began the conversation through an interpreter. We requested his authority to cross his territory, and to take a certain number of his subjects into our service, which two demands were granted before we rose.

Khama was dressed in European clothes; he is something over fifty years of age. His expression is open and benevolent; he is a refined and distinguished personality. The conversation lasted twenty minutes; he shook hands with each of us on our taking leave, and we returned to camp, following the main streets of the capital, which are lined with conical mud huts, the roofs of thatch, all protected by high palisades. Here and there groups of laughing children were at play. Mothers of families, gracefully clad in cotton garments, many carrying the last-born on their backs in a kind of sack, went by in single file to draw water, bearing amphoras upon their heads.

We had the pleasure of meeting the missionaries, M. and Mme Boiteux, of Neuchâtel, and M. Davit, from the Waldensian Valley in Piedmont, who have recently arrived, and are going to the Zambezi.

We had also the privilege of making the acquaintance of Mr. J. S. Moffat, brother-in-law to Livingstone, and son of the famous scientist and missionary, Robert Moffat,

as well as her support, in order that no alcohol of any kind might enter his country. He gained his cause. This example suffices to show the transformations that Christianity can work. *Author.*

who invented written characters for the Bechuanas, and translated the Bible into their tongue. It was he also who taught them to utilise the resources of their country as regards agriculture, to confine the springs, and irrigate the land. The Bechuanas have always been rich in oxen, milch-cows, sheep, and goats. They gather round their chiefs in the villages, where they have their fields and gardens. Beyond are vast grazing-lands; further still, on the confines or in the interior of the Kalahari, are the hunting-posts.

Bechuanaland has now come to be entirely under the political influence of England. It is divided into the Crown Colony of British Bechuanaland, which has little less than 40,000 square miles of surface, and the Bechuana Protectorate, to the north of the first, whose area is more than 250,000 square miles.

The most important tribes living under the ægis of the Protectorate, but all independently of one another, are the Bamangwato (chief, Khama), the Bakalta (chief, Linchwe), the Bakuena (chief, Sebele), the Ba-ngwaketsi (chief, Bathoen), and the Bamalete (chief, Ikaneng).

Khama, at the head of his tribe of Bamangwatos, is by far the most influential and important of these chiefs.

According to the "Official Handbook," whence I take these details of the census of 1891, the population of British Bechuanaland is only 60,333, or only one and a half inhabitants to the square mile!

As for the Protectorate, its population is not known, as no census has ever been taken; but its area of six times that of the Colony must be still more sparsely populated.

To-day these vast countries are becoming organised little by little, and without hitches, thanks to the English system of colonisation, which is practical, full of common sense, and able to adapt itself to all circumstances and places.

Before we start again, here is a summary description of our moving house, the waggon, which we are about to enter. Its dimensions are approximately as follows: Twenty feet long, or seventy feet, with its team of eight pairs of oxen; seven feet wide, and ten feet high. The wooden body rests directly on the axles, and is surmounted by a tilt of hoops covered with triple canvas. In front is a chest holding what provisions we keep to hand; I hold the key, and am responsible for it. On this chest we mount to the bedroom, shared by Reid and myself. This is a little over six feet long, a little under six feet wide, and three feet in height, so we can only enter on hands and knees. A large frame of wood criss-crossed with leather thongs supports the mattresses of cork, of which we have one apiece, with several coverlets.

On either side is a rack to hold the fire-arms and cartridge-belts; large pockets of canvas hold articles of toilet, maps, field-glasses, &c., not forgetting the necessaries of needlework, which are very useful on such an expedition as ours. On the floor, baggage and provisions. All round and underneath the waggon are placed the tool-boxes, water-vessels, &c. The kitchen utensils also are suspended on either hand, always ready for the camp fire. A large raw hide, fixed to the underframing, holds hatchets, spades, jacks, and various utensils. At the rear hang the nosebags, in which the horses receive their rations of maize three times a day.

We have received the expected telegram from the Cape; it gives us the Greenwich time, by which we are able to set our chronometers right. Everything is ready, and to-morrow, the 18th of May, we shall set out for the Zambezi, which we hope to reach in six or seven weeks' time. The direction followed is north-west. Our *personnel* now consists of thirteen men, and we have at the present moment thirty-eight draught-oxen, twelve saddle-

WOMEN BUILDING HUTS AT PALAPYE
From a photograph

horses, seventeen pack-donkeys, ten dogs, two tents, a portable canoe, one large four-wheeled waggon, two smaller two-wheeled waggons, and one transport waggon, hired for the journey to the Zambezi; this we have under a contract, and are not responsible for the team or drivers.

Here is a brief inventory of the provisions which I did not mention at the time of our departure from Mafeking twenty-five days ago, and what of the remainder we have renewed at Palapye: about 800 lbs. of mealie meal (maize flour); 1,200 lbs. of unbolted meal, more or less black in colour (Boer meal),* which will be an invaluable supplement to our diet, as well as to our men's; 1,100 lbs. of maize, to give our saddle-horses a good foundation of endurance at the first; afterwards they will have to content themselves with the herbage of the veldt.

Then, cases of various preserved foods; one of these contains lime-juice; a bag of salt, a bag of coffee, soap, and candles.

Twenty-four cases of rations, carefully prepared in Europe, and intended only for the Europeans of the expedition.

The most important provisions contained in each case of rations consist of: four pounds of oatmeal, three tins of Cham's condensed milk, two pounds of dried apples, four pounds of marmalade, one pound of preserved Danish butter, two pounds of brown sugar, one bottle of lime-juice, one bottle of coffee extract, one half-pound tin of Van Houten's cocoa, saccharine tablets as a substitute for loaf sugar, carbonate of soda and cream of tartar to make the bread rise, pepper, and soap. Each case of rations weighs forty pounds.

A large number of cartridges, small pigs of lead, powder,

* Wheat meal, but dusty and dirty. *Author.*

THE EXPEDITION EN ROUTE. *Drawn by Van Mayden*

scientific instruments, photographic apparatus and plates, travelling medicine-chests in which are to be found quinine and Wartburg's tincture, the two best antidotes against fever; they should be administered in a special manner. More kitchen and many other utensils.

We are obliged also to carry a large number of objects of barter; above all, white calico, glass beads of various colours and sizes, and blankets; for the last vestiges of civilisation will soon be lost, and in the regions of Upper Zambezia, whither we are going, money will possess no value.

CHAPTER IV

IN THE DESERT

Across Khama's country—The Great Salt Lake of Makarikari—The Land of the Thousand Vleys

OUR caravan, complete and thoroughly rested, left Palapye on the evening of May 18th. It seemed as though our waggons would break to pieces in going down the slopes of the Choping Hills, our wheels had to pass over such large and numerous stones.

May 21*st*.—After a halt of a day and a half on the banks of the Lotsani river, made to afford time for recovering five stray oxen, we set off once more.

The direction taken henceforth will be approximately north-west. We shall more or less closely skirt the desert of Kalahari.

While encamped at Kabeer we lost our first horse, "Mork," who died of the "horse-sickness" endemic in this part of Africa, a disease which seems to affect the lungs and cause blood-poisoning. Yesterday his flanks were heaving violently with fever and prostration. Thanks to a large dose of quinine, he seemed better, but several hours afterwards he fell dead while being led by hand. The first victim of the expedition.

After the evening meal the five subjects of Khama whom he authorised to accompany us, and who until now were clothed in the lightest fashion with the skins of wild beasts, asked us for clothes as an advance of their wages. They began to dress themselves as we were sitting by the fire—this one in a waistcoat, that in a pair of trousers. Their delight manifested itself in great outbursts of laughter, which finished by becoming contagious. These poor fellows are aborigines, conquered by the Bechuanas and reduced by them to slavery. Only a short time ago they were prohibited from possessing anything; all their earnings belonged by law to their masters. Khama has very greatly ameliorated their lot.

May 22nd.—Before arriving at Mabelu Pudi we called halt for breakfast. After lighting the fire we discovered that we had encroached on the dwelling of a venomous scorpion, which we were not long in unearthing and killing. It resembled a large hairy spider.

At Mabelu Pudi we found water. We remained here two days. Some shepherds came to offer us this time not only sour milk, but fresh milk also, of which we took a good quantity.

We determined our position with regard to Palapye; the chain of mountains on whose slope the capital is built reminds me of the flanks of the Jura. Between us and the Choping Hills stretches a wide wooded plain, slightly undulating, with here and there a rounded hillock or kopje.

At the summit of the hill on which we were stationed—a superb tactical position, commanding the neighbouring district—we found the remains of a wall which probably dates from the times when the Bechuanas took possession of the country. Near this we found a cactus measuring more than thirty feet in height.

We assisted Reid in taking the latitude—a thing we shall often do in future.

The Royal Geographical Society of London has confided to Captain Gibbons a sextant, artificial horizon, chronometer, prismatic compass, barometer, and hypsometer. Reid has the same assortment, his own property, besides a powerful telescope for observing occultations; and each of us, in addition, possesses compasses, thermometers, &c., so that in this matter also we are well furnished. I must also mention that Reid employs a very ingenious register, which is fitted on one of the wheels of the waggon, and indicates the number of revolutions made. By a simple calculation he obtains the exact distance covered between one camp and another.

We are joined by a second contingent of Khama's people belonging to a superior caste; they bring up our strength to sixteen men, a number which will be increased in the future.

May 24th.—On leaving Mabelu Pudi we noticed a flight of locusts, with red heads, the legs and wings barred with black and white; the trees were hung with them as if with living fruit. They destroyed all foliage in their passage.

We crossed an immense wooded plain of varied aspect, enlivened by stretches of turf still yellow from the winter and broken by hills. To the north-east no obstacle limited the horizon, and the mists of the morning gave the illusion of the ocean. The African landscape has infinite variety for him who has learned to see.

This evening, during a night march very favourable to the teams, but unhappily without a moon, the large waggon got into a deep hole and heeled over to one side. We were violently thrown to the earth, but got up without serious injury. The oxen were unyoked, and then attached to the rear of the waggon, while from the other side we all pulled on a stout rope, and so set the heavy vehicle right again.

Shortly afterwards the dogs suddenly gave tongue. We

hastened, rifle in hand, in the direction where proceeded their furious baying, and found them attacking a porcupine, which was very soon killed, though several dogs were wounded. One had two quills in his side, which we had to extract on the spot by lantern-light, an operation performed not without lamentations.

We decided to let the waggons go ahead as far as Makwa, where we hope to find water, and there bivouac for the night in order to go hunting early in the morning. A "skerm" a primitive shelter of branches—is quickly run up; the horses are tethered, and we lie down to sleep round a great fire rolled in our blankets.

May 25th. A bitterly cold wind blew all night from the south-west, and we hardly slept. At half-past five we were up, and a little later in the saddle. We rode now through the bush, now across the wide, dried-up plains, rifle in hand, keeping watch on all sides. We gave chase to a gazelle, which escaped us; later, in the course of the morning, to a gnu *(Catoblepas Gorgon)* weighing three or four hundred pounds, which in the distance looked so like a small ox as to be mistaken for one. It galloped superbly, its head between its legs. The beast was driven over to Reid's side, and shot by him—a famous addition to our *cuisine*, above all with the number of men we have to feed.

After six hours' hunting we met again in camp at Kwa, where we made a meal consisting in part of boiled porcupine.

At nightfall Pirie had not come back. We fired a number of rifle shots, as we had agreed to do in such cases, at intervals of half an hour, followed at once by a rocket with red and blue stars. This we did three times, the frightened men, to our amusement, hiding themselves under the waggon.

IN THE DESERT

At ten o'clock at night Pirie has not returned; he has certainly lost himself.

We take counsel together, and decide upon sending after him to-morrow morning, at daybreak, James, the most reliable of our men, on horseback, accompanied by two Bushmen, who have no equals at finding and following a trail.

BLUE GNU

Sketch by Van Maijlen. Specimen brought home by Author

May 26th.—Although we are under the tropics, having crossed the tropic of Capricorn some time ago, it was extremely cold last night, and some tea we left out of doors yesterday evening was found this morning as a block of ice in each glass—very different from the temperature of the daytime, when one is glad of the shade.

We were unable, with the best will in the world, to swallow our traditional bowl of oatmeal in the morning, there being too large a proportion of mud in the water;

we were also obliged to renounce the most elementary ablutions.

Pirie did not return to camp till two o'clock this afternoon. As we supposed, he took a false trail yesterday while hunting, and has been twenty-seven hours without food and seventeen without water!

May 27th.—At our halt for breakfast, the gnu steaks were pronounced excellent. We encountered a party of Zambezians returning to their country after having served in the diamond mines at Kimberley. They were very picturesque in their get-up, a mixture of European and native garments. Each was armed with a rifle, and they had an air of prosperity that did one good to see. The dancer of the party, wearing a pointed head-dress capped by a long feather, came to enliven our repast. He began to dance on the spot, whistling and singing, and rattling a calabash in his right hand, a little bell dangling at his side. The water with which we have had to content ourselves to-day, and of which we found very little, is the worst we have used hitherto. We boiled it, and three times skimmed off a greenish foam, but despite this operation we had nothing to make our tea and prepare our meal with but a mixture of mud and water, with which we had to be content.

May 28th.—Tlalamabili wells: we were glad to be able to water the cattle, which had been thirsting for thirty-nine hours! To control the impatience of the poor beasts, and to see that the weaker ones had their share, we led them to the water a few at a time—not without difficulty. We continued our journey along a sandy trail, through a country in which the trees grew larger and more numerous, in order to arrive in the course of the day at the camp of Linokaneng, rejoicing in the thought

WE ADVANCE PAINFULLY

Drawn by Bandier, from a photograph by the Author

of finding there pure and abundant water. But no such thing. Certainly it was no longer liquid mud that we found, but, alas! water of a grey colour, which we were glad enough to get.

We were surrounded by splendid trees, and there was no lack of sand-grouse in the neighbourhood—one of the best game-birds of this part of Africa.

The aspect of the country we are traversing is changing continually; our march to-day led us through a wooded valley, surrounded by hills with flattened summits, a veritable ocean of foliage, checkered with green and yellow. The greater number of these trees were *mopani* trees, whose leaves, divided in two parts, have the shape of a pair of butterfly's wings. They were interspersed with terrible thickets of various species of thorns, of which the most formidable is the *wacht-een-beetje*, appropriately interpreted as the "wait-a-bit"; a crooked, steely, regular fish-hook of a thorn, that stops and tears everything that comes in its way. I have been almost pulled out of the saddle by one of these "wait-a-bit" thickets!

May 30th.—Travelling through open country we reached the south-east of Makarikari.

The Makarikari lake is a salt lake some sixty miles long, and in the present season it is for the greater part dried up. The natives come here to gather salt on its banks. We went hunting antelope on horseback across its bed of cracked salt. We were deceived by a mirage: we saw the appearance of great sheets of clear water in the distance, which receded as we approached.

From the midst of the grasses in which we encamped rose round anthills, inhabited by ants whose red heads are armed with a spike. The interiors of these anthills are wonderfully made; our men opened them and made them serve as bread-ovens.

We received a visit from three Masaroa, the natives of these parts. The youngest wore a diadem of glass beads, and a number of necklets and bracelets, the predominating colour being blue.

We encountered also a party of Zambezians going to take service at Kimberley. Thin, suspicious, possessing nothing but their calabashes hung at the end of their long staffs, they contrasted strikingly with those we met returning to their homes after having worked for several years in a civilised country.

The district we are passing through is moderately wooded, and harbours numbers of guinea-fowl which, as every one knows, are excellent game.

May 31*st.*—We reached the wells of Kariba, and were able to water the beasts, which had had nothing to drink since the muddy water of yesterday evening. I am often speaking of water—it is one of our greatest pre-occupations—where shall we find it, and what sort of water will it be? The few natives we meet do not, as a rule, choose to give us exact information on the subject.

June 1*st.*—An excellent meal of broiled antelope and guinea-fowl; in the afternoon we gave chase to a troop of ostriches.

June 2*nd.*—We camped last night on the banks of the Simoane river. Its waters, like those of many other rivers, are absorbed by the Makarikari, and are unfortunately muddy.

We had the good fortune to come across the camp of Sekhomi, only son of Khama, who was returning from the north with a large following. He said he had killed eleven giraffes. His six waggons were ranged in a line along the riverside. We dismounted and shook hands,

He is a man of twenty-five or thirty, tall and supple; he speaks several words of English.

He visited our camp in the course of the day, riding in on horseback with several followers. He brought us a fat sheep, and expressed his thanks when we offered him sugar and coffee. The sheep is welcome, and will make a pleasant change, as the staple of our diet has been game for some time past.

Sekhomi, who is returning to Palapye, is good enough to carry our letters.

We shall reach the banks of the Nata (Matangwe) river presently.

June 3rd.—Last night, it being fine and clear, we skirted the north-east angle of the great salt lake, Makarikari, which at this season is partly dry. Beneath our feet is a vast whitish waste; above our heads the blue of the sky. In the evening we halt near the confluence of the Shua and Nata rivers—both of them absorbed by the Makarikari. Here we shall rest for a day or two.

There is not much meat in the camp; we must take this into consideration. We have sixteen mouths to feed, exclusive of our own—and what appetites! We give our men two pounds of maize flour daily, a ration which is withheld and replaced by meat on hunting days. Result: a saving of thirty-two pounds of flour in twenty-four hours.

June 4th.—We were in the saddle by six o'clock in the morning, and set out hunting. The sun was hot already when we reached a Masaroa village, or rather a few wattle huts (thatched with dry grasses, and more like haystacks than anything else) scattered among the trees, with here and there a "skerm." In one of the latter we

HUNTING GNUS. *Drawn by Van Muyden*

found eight Masaroa grouped round the fire—probably the notabilities of the district. One of them, the chief, who was still a young man, seemed to be held in great respect by his companions.

These Masaroa were scantily covered by a few skins of wild beasts; all of them wore various ornaments of glass pearls or metal work: ear-rings, bracelets, necklaces, &c. One of the oldest wore two copper buttons of European make in his ears, while another had made himself a bracelet of a number of little white buttons. Several had in addition amulets hanging from their necks, also a long cobbler's awl in a wooden sheath; the latter they use to extract thorns from their feet.

The chief, armed with a club and a lance, took the head of our column, followed by three of his subjects. Soon he began to examine the ground on all hands for traces of game. For some time his eyes left the earth only to scrutinise the horizon. After a long march he climbed a tree, and gave us to understand that he had a herd of gnus in sight. Rifles in hand, we directed our horses at a walk in the direction given. The gnus became visible against the yellowish grass; we began to distinguish them more clearly; they were grazing to the number of thirty. No sooner had we come within a few hundred yards of them, than the whole herd broke into a sudden gallop. We did the same. The whole herd being thoroughly scared, the beasts made circles and detours, which we endeavoured to cut. They raised clouds of dust, like a cavalry charge. After a hot chase of a few miles across the immense dry grass-plain, we were certain of procuring fresh meat for ourselves and our men.

Pirie, Reid, and myself presently set off in the direction of the river, and Captain Gibbons endeavoured to follow several isolated gnus.

WE ENCAMP UNDER AN "ACACIA GIRAFFA"

Drawn by Londier, from a photograph by the Author

June 5th.—They led him further than he expected, for it was daylight when he returned to the camp. He had to lead his horse the greater part of the way back, and to content himself with a solitary supper off the tongue of the beast he had killed, afterwards sleeping without blankets *à la belle étoile*.

June 6th.—We had to ford the Nata river. The oxen were scarcely up to their knees in water, but, to judge by the height and width of the banks, it cannot be an easy ford in the rainy season. A little while ago the pole of our second waggon broke, and had to be repaired without delay. We were following a sandy trail which gave our teams much trouble; a dense cloud of dust enveloped us, and penetrated everything. At other times we rode through the midst of tall russet grasses, in which our horses disappeared up to their manes; finally across a country of gentle undulations covered with thorn-thickets of various heights.

June 7th.—We passed the day by the Horns-Vley pool, and established our camp under a great tree (*Acacia Giraffa*). One of the oxen, which had dislocated its shoulder, had to be killed. The men have been actively occupied in preparing *biltong*, cutting the meat into thin strips, which are sprinkled with salt and dried in the open air; they can be kept thus for a long time.

One must have a great experience of life in this part of Africa to be able, while looking after the teams, and keeping them in good health, to get out of them all the work they can do. Of the members of our expedition, Gibbons and Reid especially possess this experience, and we have so far had good results in the matters of health and distance covered. It is no slight thing to organise the "treks," to know when to travel by night, and to

IN THE BUSH
From a photograph by the Author

calculate distance so as to find water at the places of halt.

We have apportioned the work in such a manner that, while the whole of us work together as well as possible, each has his special function.

June 13th.—Here we are at the Tamasetsie pool. A giraffe was killed yesterday; we shall stay here till to-morrow. The men are preparing *biltong* for our use from the white flesh, one of the best meats one can eat, especially when cut from a young animal.

For several days now we have had no lack of water; we are crossing the country called the "Land of the Thousand Vleys," a region of thousands of ponds and lakes; depressions of the soil in which the precious liquid is found, at this season, in satisfying quantities, though of varying quality.

From Horns-Vley we have been following a trail of heavy sand, which tires the teams badly. This track is for the greater part bordered by thickets, to pass which the waggons have often only just room; here and there we have to cut down a tree. It is an ordeal for the drivers. Each team has its special driver, who goes continually from place to place, armed with a great whip. In moments of difficulty he addresses himself to individual oxen (and each has its name) without rest or truce, now in invective, now in encouragement, in a piercing voice of infinite variations. He is seconded by the leader, who marches in front of the foremost yoke of oxen.

At the moment of inspanning—an interesting operation to watch—the leader receives from the driver the order to round up the oxen grazing near by. He in his turn, with the help of the other "boys," places the oxen in single file before the waggon, on the left of the long iron chain which runs from the pole, to which the yokes

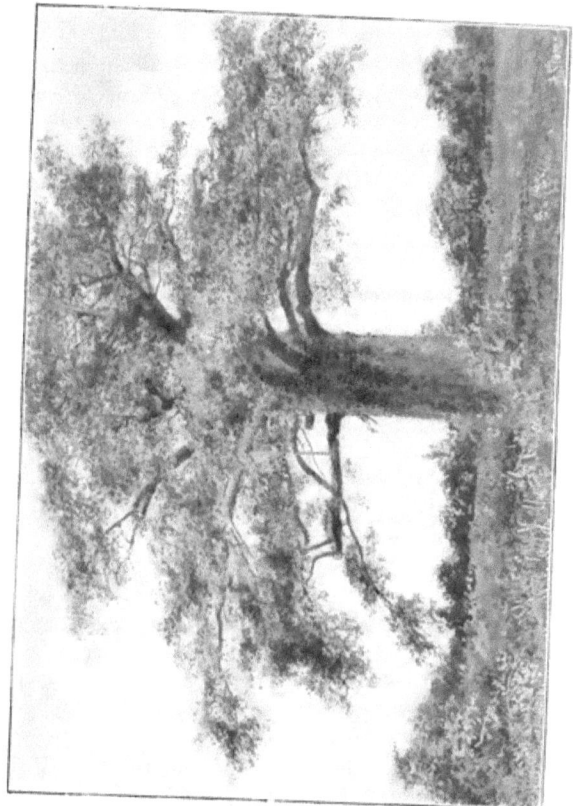

A BAOBAB
From a photograph by the Author

are fastened by the middle. The driver, with the help of his men, passes a leather thong round the horns of each beast, and then chooses his pairs, which are led to the right-hand side of the chain, where each pair is made to face its respective yoke. The latter is then placed on the necks of the pair, each neck being checked by two light slips of wood fixed to the yoke. The sixteen or eighteen cattle of the large waggon are in this manner yoked in a few minutes, though not without plenty of shouting.

June 16*th*.—We called a halt at "Lake Baobab." A splendid baobab tree, measuring nearly twenty-six feet in circumference, rises by the bank. The strong canvas tilt of the large waggon had been torn by thorns, and was in urgent need of repair. We made an excellent breakfast off roasted giraffe tongue and steaks.

The day before yesterday we chased a herd of zebras on horseback. During the last few days we have, on several occasions, found the old spoor of elephants, and fresh ones of lions.

After leaving "Baobab Lake" we once more traversed clearings and sandy tracks alternating with harder soil; an undulating district.

We crossed the watershed which divides the Zambezi on the north from the Limpopo on the south. This watershed is 3,000 to 3,500 feet above sea-level.

In considering the appearance of this country, one cannot help asking one's self if the theory started, I think, by Livingstone, is not correct—*i.e.*, that the country between the Zambezi and Shoshong* formed originally a great lake or inland sea, which became reduced to the Makarikari of to-day when another out-

* Formerly a capital; to-day abandoned by Khama, chief of the Bamangwato. It was not far from Palapye. *Author*.

let was formed in the direction of the Indian Ocean, in the place now known as the Victoria Falls.

June 17th.—On reaching the Daka river, reduced at present to its lowest level, we came upon the camp of three Englishmen. Before we had time to decline our respective names and qualities we found ourselves sharing their lunch. How hearts are expanded and hands held out when Europeans meet unexpectedly in these immense solitudes! *

These gentlemen, of whom two are mining engineers, have been sent out by a syndicate to prospect the soil bordering on the Gway river, a southern affluent of the Zambezi, with a view to mining operations. What interesting details they gave us! It was nightfall before we thought of putting foot in stirrup to rejoin our waggons, which had gone ahead; but an hour of rapid riding brought us in sight of our great camp fires.

They offered us a present of inestimable value: a stewpan! The three utensils of this kind that we possessed were broken long ago in our rough-and-ready life. We also had the satisfaction of eating good bread: the one of our "boys" who fulfils the functions of baker can only turn out a material heavy as lead with the unbolted meal which he employs.

Good bread and drinkable water—two things one must have been deprived of to appreciate at their true value!

These three gentlemen had no sextant among their instruments. We gave them the latitude of their camp by means of ours.

The British S. A. Chartered Company seems to aspire to great things in these parts.

* Since our return we have learned of the death of two of these gentlemen. *Author.*

We have at several points of our route struck on the territory formerly re-taken by Lobengula, the king of the Matabele, an unspeakably cruel race of robbers, showing no mercy to their prisoners, and the terror of the surrounding tribes, on whom the Colonial arms inflicted a terrible lesson in 1893.

June 18th.—From the Daka river we travelled northwest across a range of hills; then along a valley which led us, shortly after passing the bed of the Matetsi river, to Panda-Matenga. From this tableland we had in the direction of the Zambezi an extensive outlook upon the neighbouring country, an immense plain crossed by undulating woodlands, whose sombre foliage contrasted with the clear light tones of the plain. At Panda-Matenga we saw mud huts again for the first time since leaving Palapye. During the whole journey we have met with nothing but a few miserable hovels built of boughs and dried grass, inhabited by Bushmen and Masaroa.

DUIKER,
"CEPHALOPHUS MERGENS."
Sketch by Van Maydell.
Specimen brought home by Author.

We are celebrating a birthday to-night. During the day we were fortunate enough to buy part of a kid; a welcome change in our diet, of which the staple has been for several days, giraffe flesh prepared in the most various manners.

June 19th.—We camped in the veldt at Gazuma-Vley, where we established "kraals." To this place, once we are on the banks of the Zambezi, we shall send back the oxen and part of the horses; these, together with the waggons, we shall leave in the charge of several trustworthy men. The latter will remain here, while we, after crossing the river, shall penetrate Borotsi. At Gazuma-Vley there is water in abundance, and the tsetse fly,

A DINNER
Drawn by Thiriat, from a photograph

whose bite means certain death to domestic animals, in a longer or shorter time, need not be feared. These kraals are spaces surrounded with boughs of thorn-trees, which must be close enough and high enough to keep out all wild beasts. The horses and oxen will be shut up in them every night.

Our hunting battery consists of five express rifles and

four smooth-bores, all arms of the first quality. I have also brought with me a Swiss cavalry carbine, 1893 model, and we have in addition several Männlicher rifles (a cavalry arm of the latest model).

June 20th.— We came across a great many spoor of wild beasts—giraffe, zebra, &c. This country should be a good one for game. I had the good luck to kill for our larder a duiker (*Cephalophus mergens*), an antelope, affording excellent meat.

While chasing a troop of tsessebe antelopes (*Alcephalus lunatus*) Pirie had a fall from his horse. This accident is inevitable, and has happened to all of us, for these prairies are honeycombed by an infinite number of holes dug by a species of ant-eater. It is impossible to avoid these holes when going at full gallop. Pirie came off with a bruised foot.

June 21st. We followed a sandy track through the forest, where we noticed some orchids.

Reid and I have decided to reconnoitre on horseback in the direction of the Zambezi. Reid carries a carbine, I the teapot and bag of provisions.

CHAPTER V

THE ZAMBEZI

On the banks of the River—Kazungula, in Borotsi.

WE took to the saddle on June 22nd, shortly after midnight. We descended the valley insensibly towards Leshoma. There was no moon; nothing is more unpleasant, when equipped in our fashion, than to gallop across country in darkness.

At daybreak we were saluted by the very unmusical cries of a colony of monkeys, which had set up house in the foliage of a splendid mimosa, and at six o'clock we came out upon the banks of the great river. For the time being the water was shrouded in a thick mist, and all we could perceive of Borotsiland,[*] on the other bank, was the missionary station, and the thatched huts of the native village of Kazungula.

After warming ourselves at a fire—lit with difficulty on account of the heavy dew—we fired shots to attract the

[*] After having consulted M. Coillard, a high authority on the matter, having lived nearly forty years in Africa, I have adopted in this book the rules proposed by him concerning the orthography of the names of the various territories, tribes, or peoples, found in the kingdom of the ba-Rotsi. The prefixes "ba" or "ma" indicate the plural, the prefix "mo" is used in the singular to indicate an individual; the prefix "bo" indicates the country itself. Thus: the ba-Rotsi—a mo-Rotsi—the bo-Rotsi country. These prefixes represent in some sort the article, and take a small initial while the proper name itself is

attention of a native boatman who was passing along the opposite bank. He finally answered our signals. We watched him coming; he wore a loin-cloth and stood upright in his canoe, which was a long, narrow dug-out. We found there was just room to sit down, and were soon set ashore in the kingdom of the Barotsi.

We knocked at the door of the missionaries, M. and Mme Louis Jalla, natives of the Waldensian Valley in Piedmont, who gave us the most cordial welcome, and there and then made us sit down to table. They were good enough to give us much valuable news, and we left them regretfully in the afternoon to cross back again to the right bank of the Zambezi, there to saddle up our horses and set out to meet our waggons, which we rejoined in the evening at Leshoma.

June 23rd–24th.—Two days have been devoted to taking an inventory of our stores, and to dividing them into easily portable loads, which had to be weighed out. We are leaving behind everything that might encumber us, as well as some provisions which we shall find on our return. All the oxen which are not indispensable are sent back to Gazuma-Vley, together with most of the horses; then, taking all necessaries with us, we make our last stage in order to arrive at the river by night, so as to protect the oxen from the tsetse fly, which infests these parts.

written with a capital. Referring to the authority cited above, I have employed the same rules in writing the names of tribes or people living to the south of the Zambezi, except in some cases where the name has already been Gallicised. *Author.*

I have for the most part adhered to the phonetic transliteration of Capt. Bertrand's, or rather M. Coillard's, orthography of these names, with the one exception of transferring the capital to the prefix, as has already been done in Anglicising other South African names, as— Matabele, Mashona, &c. *Trans.*

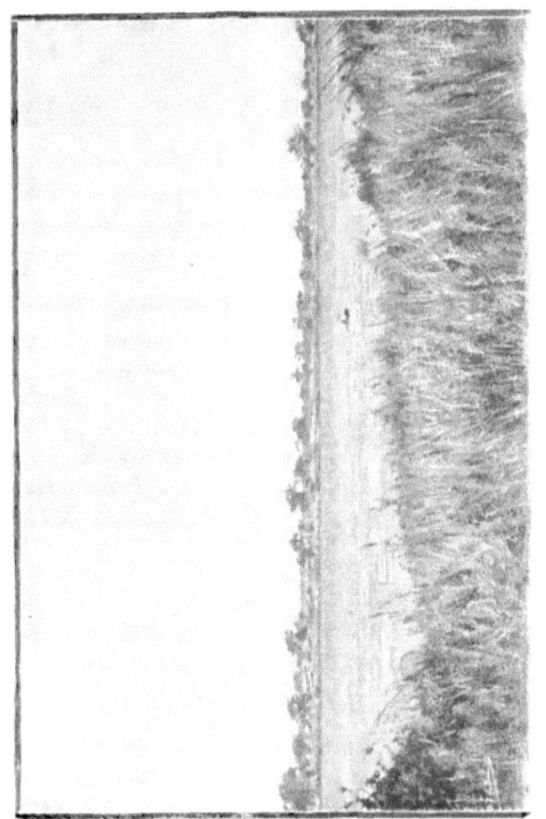

THE ZAMBEZI NEAR ITS CONFLUENCE WITH THE LINYANTI
Drawn by Fondier, from a photograph by the Author

The night of the 24th was the last passed in the waggons. Early the next morning we pitched our tents on the right bank of the Zambezi. We found time, although working hard, to admire the spectacle before us during these two days. The waters of this splendid river, which, in the neighbourhood of our camp, measures four or five hundred yards in width, roll onward as blue as are those of Lake Leman at this season of the year. On the right side, and flowing somewhat in the same direction, the Chobe river (Linyanti) * forms its confluence with the Zambezi. This river is dotted with many islands: the natives call themselves Liambae. Here and there a slender palm gives the tropical note. From time to time black cormorants, or heavy-flying geese, pass through the air overhead. Opposite us, on the left bank, Kazungula stands out upon a background of foliage.

June 25th. After breakfasting we placed our canoe on the water for the first time. It is of sail-cloth, in sections, water-proofed with rubber, portable, and weighs 160 lbs. We crossed the Zambezi. Thanks to the kindness of M. and Mme Louis Jalla, we were enabled immediately to buy 1,300 or 1,400 lbs. of sorghum, maize, millet, and ground-nuts; but we had to transport all this cargo to the other bank. Unhappily the wind had risen, the river was choppy, and the native boatmen refused to work under these conditions. On the other hand, time was pressing, and it was an urgent matter that the beasts should be returned in the evening to Gazuma-Vley in order to escape the tsetse fly.

As our boat, the *Zambezia*, answered well, we decided in the course of the morning to effect the transport ourselves, taking the paddles in turn; a plan certainly not without risk. All went well, however, and at the ap-

* It is also called the Quando. *Trans.*

pointed time our last waggon resumed the road to Gazuma-Vley, with the provisions for the three men forming our rearguard, who are to tend the oxen and horses while awaiting our return.

M. Jalla gives us the good news that King Lewanika, in answer to the request made him some months ago, has sent us from his capital, Lealuyi, authority to enter, with arms and baggage, his kingdom of Borotsiland.

CHAPTER VI

IN THE KINGDOM OF THE BAROTSI—THE RIVER MACHILI

To Kazungula—We follow the course of the Machili—We reach the source of the Machili, in the territory of the Mankoya tribe.

THE Zambezi has returned to its usual aspect. Early on June 26th Prince Litia, who is the king's eldest son, and the governor of this part of the country, put four canoes with their crews at our disposal, under a Zambezian chief. The latter held in his hands a short black staff, the badge of his authority. The work of the day consisted in transporting our stores to the left bank of the Zambezi, to say nothing of a score of asses, and the four horses we are taking with us on this part of the journey. The only possible way of getting our beasts to the other bank was to put them into the water by force, one by one; they swam beside or behind the canoe, held by the bridle. Then came the turn of the stores, and then that of our men, we ourselves crossing last.

June 27th.—The business of transport came to an end last night without mishap, and we are encamped for the first time on the territory of Lewanika, King of the Barotsi. Toby, our favourite dog, was the only creature that did not answer our call, and we imagine he must have been snapped up by a crocodile while drinking at the river. These hideous amphibians are to all accounts guilty of many graver misdeeds than this, so we were fortunate in our passages yesterday.

The hereditary prince Litia, who lives at Kazungula, came accompanied by M. Jalla to visit our camp, which is pitched near the missionary station. Litia inspires sympathy at once with his pleasant smile and simple manner. He is a man of great moral worth, and is openly a convert to Christianity. This victory is due

THE MISSIONARY STATION OF M. AND MME. LOUIS JALLA
Drawn by Boudier, from a photograph by the Author

to the representations of MM. Coillard and Jalla, who have been the instruments of God in educating this man, to-day in the flower of his age; and in him, being as he is in a high position, reposes in great part the hope of the mission. We have information from perfectly reliable sources that his conduct is in complete accord with his Christian convictions. An active and intelligent man, he loves to seek relaxation in working in wood and iron. At present he is building himself a new house, directing the work himself.

While paying a call directly after our arrival, I admired the neatness of his thatch palace, in which the Bible, well in evidence, occupied the place of honour.

I was also present at class in the native school organised by Mme Jalla and Mlle Kiener. The latter, a native of Dombresson, in the canton of Neuchâtel, is M. and Mme Jalla's right hand. I was struck at once by the perfect order and discipline which reigned in the school; an order and discipline the more remarkable as by force of circumstances the pupils are of the most various ages.

There was a big, bearded young man seated in the infant school; he was very anxious to learn, his eyes attentively perusing the blackboards. Certainly these ladies could not arrive at such results, and hold everybody so well in hand, but for their great patience, the fruit of their extreme piety, and a special gift in education. I heard hymns sung which, in accuracy and feeling, would have done credit to any European Sunday school.

June 28th.—For several days we have all been busy and animated in the camp, with a view to continuing the journey. This will now be made in a totally different manner, consequent on the nature of the country to be traversed. We have twenty-five pack donkeys, and the excess of stores will be carried by porters in lots of not more than fifty pounds weight; so these we have to calculate, divide, and weigh. Then we have to lay in the necessary provisions for our men, whose number will be increased.

There has been a famine in the district recently, but M. Jalla, with his unfailing kindness, was once more of great help to us in spreading the news that we wanted to purchase. Natives came from long distances to sell us their produce: millet, sorghum, maize, beans of various kinds, and ground-nuts, which they carried in calabashes slung over the shoulder at the ends of a long staff. There are several fine types among these Zambezians, who squat motionless at a respectful distance; time seems to have

LEAVING SCHOOL AT KAZUNGULA
From a photograph by the Author

no value for them. The standard of currency employed in our transactions is the ell of white calico.

June 29th.—Very busy. M. and Mme Louis Jalla are making things easy for us. Although their two children are ill, they insist on our lunching with them — a hospitality one or another of us has accepted on several occasions.

  ° The ell of white calico, or *setsiba*, is usually measured along the arm, from the shoulder to the finger-ends.—*Author*.

Sunday, June 30th.—I was present at the mission-church this morning, at the service held for the natives by M. Jalla. I remarked the quietness and the sustained attention of the congregation—about 200 men, women, and children—as well as the manner in which the hymns were sung. I was sitting not far from Prince Litia, who at the conclusion of the service prayed that his father King Lewanika might not merely encourage missionary work in his country, as he has done for a long time past, but become himself sincerely converted to the Gospel. Lewanika, it appears, is agreeable, but up to the present the question of polygamy has prevented his taking the decisive step.

The history of this missionary station, intimately connected with the birth of the village of Kazungula, is a remarkable one. In 1889, M. and Mme Louis Jalla, who had for several years previously preached the Gospel at Sesheke, some miles up-river, came hither to found this station, to-day so flourishing. Its site was then a maize-field. In 1892 King Lewanika ordered one of his chiefs, Makumba, to see to the establishment of a village beside the missionary station. The thatched huts multiplied one by one until to-day the station contains an approximate population of 600, of whom 115 men and women have already expressed their desire to renounce their pagan customs. In all probability the place will contain a thousand inhabitants before long. After Lealuyi, the capital, it is considered the most important centre of the kingdom, being the one from which all news radiates; it is also the key to Borotsi.

The chief Makumba has died since our arrival. According to custom he was buried by night a few hours afterwards. His wives having mourned for him three days, their heads were shaven, and the various huts belonging to him were razed to the ground; we saw

PRINCE LITTA LEAVING THE CHAPEL.
From a photograph by the Author

their remains yesterday. One of his wives, who was accused of sorcery, and threatened with being cast into the river, came to the mission for refuge, where she was received and fed. No one has dared to seek to take her away by force ; such is the prestige among these savages of these few men and women, slaves to duty, who would not even defend themselves if attacked.

Mme Jalla has in her house (this and the church were constructed entirely by her husband) ten young native girls, whom she is so training as to become, in the future, mothers of families able to bring up their children in turn, and to possess a home-life. It appears the same is being done at other stations.

Prince Litia attended worship this afternoon ; at his approach, in accordance with the etiquette of the Barotsi, his subjects squatted on their heels and softly clapped their hands.

Monday, July 1st.—We have to-day had the pleasure of the company of M. and Mme Jalla, Mlle Kiener, and the Rev. Mr. Buckenham to lunch in our camp. The last named is a missionary in the Moshukulumbwe country.*

In order to disembarrass ourselves, and to be able to advance rapidly, we have left behind everything that might encumber us—such as camp chairs and tables. On the occasion of this invitation we had recourse to the cases of rations as a substitute. Nine of them formed the table ; others, covered with our best blankets in honour of the ladies, made very presentable seats.

Some minutes before our guests arrived we sent them a messenger, asking them to be good enough to bring knives and forks. The lunch, a creation of Reid's, was

---

* Mr. Buckenham died at Kazungula on July 11, 1896. *Author.*

pronounced excellent. It was a farewell feast. The menu comprised ragoût d'antilope, with carrots and dried potatoes and marmalade, and a so-called rice pudding. The stimulants appropriate to such occasions were replaced by the moderately cool water of the Zambezi, and by tea and coffee.

Our preparations are over; we must start. It will not be easy to forget these few days passed at Kazungula by the mission station; its pleasant aspect, the cordial welcome received, and the healthful atmosphere breathed made it a veritable oasis in the desert.

We shall set out to-morrow in a northerly direction, our destination being the Machili river, whose source we wish to reach. We are twenty-five strong, and we shall make reinforcements as we proceed. We have twenty-five pack donkeys, six dogs, and four saddle-horses; the latter, in all probability, will have to be sacrificed.

Captain Gibbons goes westward up the course of the Zambezi, on a different exploration from ours. We hope to meet again later.

July 2nd.—The last inspection before leaving Kazungula was held at two o'clock in the afternoon. The loads, already weighed out, were distributed to the men, who were patiently sitting on their heels, and came forward one by one as their names were called to receive their respective lots of about fifty pounds weight; these they carry on their shoulders, balanced in two portions at the ends of a long staff. The donkeys have their pack-saddles put on, and are loaded to the extent of eighty-five to a hundred and twenty pounds. Then we mount our horses, and the caravan begins to wind across the great plain.

These first days, before each man thoroughly knows what is expected of him, and above all before men and beasts are inured to fatigue, are a trying time. Moreover, the packs of the donkeys are lashed with cords made of plaited grass, which are constantly breaking. As soon as we kill any big game we shall make good solid thongs out of the hide. All our available patience is necessary, when we see, all over the place, here a bale and there a packing-case thrown to the ground, and the disembarrassed animal, delighted at being quit of his burden, fleeing at full gallop.

We call a halt in a wood of mopani trees. The tent is pitched hastily, the loads set down in line, and here comes Jonnes, the cook, with the welcome news that " the table is served."

This phrase is just a little pretentious, for, as I have said, we left everything that might embarrass us at Kazungula together with the last traces of civilisation, and henceforth our table and chairs are mother earth.

July 3rd.—Afoot before sunrise, we strike camp immediately. Two horses have strayed in the night; Pirie and I have to await the return of the men sent on their trail. After this delay we pass by the village of Mombewa, a mere handful of huts, and see the inhabitants in the distance. Great heat; we camp near the Intangwe river.

July 4th. After having experienced the same difficulties as on the preceding days, we pass the night on the banks of the Umgwezi river. Three of our men get hurts on the march. Once more, in tending them, I have occasion to put into practice the excellent directions given by the doctor who founded the Samaritan's work in Geneva.

July 5th.—Rising in the dark, we started very early,

wishing to reach the Kasaia river to-day. We passed alternately through plains and wooded spaces, where we saw several superb baobab trees. We reached our destination in the course of the afternoon; the last of the men joined us at seven o'clock at night, and we decided to call a halt of two days here, for we absolutely must have some raw-hide thongs, to say nothing of meat for the lot of us. We have recruited eight new porters *en route*, making thirty-three men to feed, exclusive of ourselves.

REEDBUCK, "CERVICAPRA ARUNDINACEA"
Sketch by Van Muyden. Specimen brought home by the Author

July 6th. We killed a zebra and a gnu; I for my part added two reedbucks to our larder, antelopes of elegant shape (*Cervicapra arundinacea*), and excellent eating. All hands that can be spared are busily employed in preparing *biltong* and in making thongs of hide.

We are in the lion country; according to report there is a very dangerous lioness with her cubs in our neighbourhood; a negro just escaped falling a victim to her the day before our arrival.

July 7th.—Sunday; a day of rest. The dogs last night were not quiet for a moment; the horses and asses, penned up in their usual kraal of branches, showed great uneasiness; there were beasts of prey prowling round the camp.

After supper, Pirie was calmly smoking his pipe beside the fire, when he was suddenly cast out of his beatitude by the sting of a scorpion, which was probably brought in among the faggots. These noxious creatures often

LIVINGSTONE'S ELAND, "OREAS CANNA."
Sketch by Van Maydên. Specimen brought home by the Author.

lodge themselves between the bark and the wood, until the heat drives them from their refuge.

July 8th.—After a night as unquiet as the preceding one, we made the porters, in the first hours of the day, carry the loads of the pack-asses down to the right bank of the Kasaia river, whose banks are very steep; at this season the river is easily forded. The donkeys, which

have a decided dislike to water, were taken over one by
one, not without a desperate resistance. We resumed
our march through a fine growth of palm and baobab,
and passed a troop of gnus which were unsuspiciously
grazing.

July 9th.—We encamped on the right bank of the
Machili river, an affluent of the Zambezi which, as I
stated before, we intend to follow to its source. This
river is only dotted down in the best geographical charts,
so that we are in an unexplored region.

During this last march we called a halt near a village
surrounded with plantations of millet, maize, and gourds.
We noticed some platforms raised a few feet above the
ground, on which the women were engaged in husking
maize. Domestic animals were represented by small
black and white goats, poultry, and sheep with large
tails. Our men, tired of the animal food which forms
almost exclusively their daily diet, exchanged some of
the venison served out to them for ground-nuts and
millet.

Two of our porters, who unknown to us had remained
at the rear of the column, abandoned their loads and ran
away. An expedition might be very seriously embarrassed if, as has happened before on other expeditions, the
porters were to desert *en masse*. We hope that this, if
we take all precautions, will not be our fate. For the
rest, we have a certain number of Bechuanas, Bushmen,
and Masaroa, who here across the Zambezi are very far
from their homes; they have shared our cares and
pleasures for a long time; but if they were to abandon us
we should have the donkeys as a last resource.

Reid, who was in advance, killed an eland *Oreas canna*,
a powerful beast, which, unlike other species of antelope,
has not a rapid gait. Its weight must be fully a thousand

pounds; the shoulder alone weighs eighty. The meat of the *Oreas canna* reminds one of beef. Its fat is valuable, for we can employ it without too much repugnance for cooking purposes.

Our men are making thongs with the hide of the big game killed lately. As a substitute for tanning they proceed as follows: After cutting, on the carcase, bands of an inch or two in width and as long as possible, they pass one or more such thongs over the branch of a tree overhead, and join the ends. Suspended in the loop thus formed they place a heavy stone, and above this, outside the thongs, two strong sticks fastened at the ends. By means of these sticks, singing all the while, they twist the thongs till they can twist no more, and let them untwist of themselves, repeating the process until the hide reaches the desired degree of pliability.

At this spot the Machili might be about 300 yards or more in width, to judge by its banks, but the stream is at present at its lowest and very feeble. During the rainy season there must be a considerable volume of water.

Up to the present we have sighted many wild animals either isolated or in small groups. For several days now we cross a zone wherein we encounter gnus and zebras by hundreds—a splendid sight. These two species would seem to have a marked predilection for one another, and are often seen in company. There is nothing more interesting than to observe the manner of living of these animals in their native wilds. The zebras appear to mount guard with great sagacity; so soon as they see anything unusual, or hear the least sound, they range themselves in the open like veritable sentinels.

While following up this portion of the Machili, the appearance of the soil gives one to suppose that a great part of the country adjacent to the river must be more or less inundated by the waters in the rainy season.

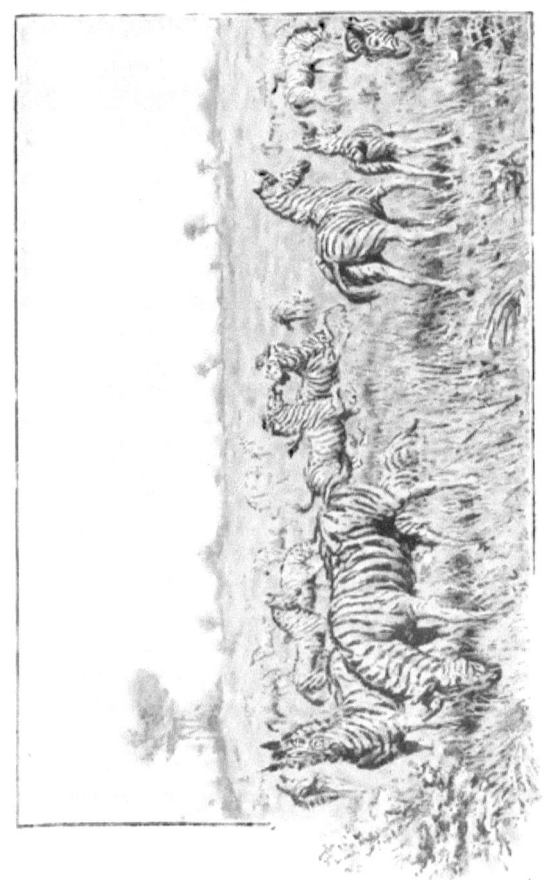

HERD OF ZEBRA NEAR THE MACHILI

Drawn by Van Ingen

Our rest of nights has often been disturbed by the laughing of hyenas prowling around the camp; the dogs reply with energy.

July 12th.—After we were once more on the march, and just making another halt, our men killed a serpent, apparently venomous, eight feet in length, a few paces from the tent. They brought us some fish and some water-tortoises. We pitched our camp on an elevated piece of ground surrounded with dwarf palm-trees; the place must be an island during the rains. We sighted some lechwe (*Cobus leche*), antelopes with long hoofs; they live by preference in moist places. For several days we have heard the grunting of hippopotami. I saw one of these animals disappear while I was skirting the river; he was replaced after a few minutes by a crocodile, whose hideous head only emerged from the water. Here and there great wading birds were promenading, seeming not the least in the world surprised at our presence.

July 16th.—We camped on the great plain, in other words the river-bed, where at this time of the dry season there are only shallow tortuous

SNAKE KILLED ON THE MARCH. *Size, one-twentieth nature, by the Author.*

The structure of this serpent interests us. The head is small, the body tapers gradually to a point scarcely larger than a knitting-needle. I have preserved the skin, although our men showed much repugnance to taking it off. *Author.*

CAMP NEAR THE MACHILI
From a photograph by the Author

streams. But we had to be cautious, for the reeds and aquatic plants often conceal holes where one may easily founder—an experience we have often undergone.

Klass Africa, an old elephant-hunter whom we have engaged for a time, joined us here. He will fulfil the functions of a sub-officer over our men. Like Jonnes, the cook, he is of Hottentot origin, a yellow man. He is accompanied by three native servants, who every night construct a "skerm" for him, wherein he sleeps with his rifle always ready to hand. He is a man of resource, and entirely self-sufficient.

We were enjoying a moment's repose in the afternoon, when suddenly a pair of lions was signalled in the neighbourhood of the camp. We jumped for our guns and pursued them through the thorny scrub. Reid had the good fortune to kill the lioness at close quarters; the writhing beast still found strength enough to wound Swatt, a spaniel, the pluckiest of dogs. It took four men to carry the carcase, and great was the joy of our men, who formed up in an escort, singing a chant of victory, repeating as refrain: "The great chief is dead; he will return no more."

This magnificent lioness measures eight feet two inches from the tip of the muzzle to the end of the tail; from the tread of the paw to the shoulder its height is thirty-two inches; its girth is forty-three inches, and the canine teeth of the upper jaw are an inch and three-quarters long. What strikes us above all, now that the beast is skinned, is the strength of the fore-limbs and the size of the paws, which are armed with talons like claws of steel.

July 17th.—Yesterday's victory was dearly bought. In the night two of our horses, Reid's and mine, were killed by the companion of the lioness. Poor "Help," so keen

and so lively, I did not think yesterday I was mounting you for the last time!

The traces of the lion allowed us to track him, but the scrub was so thick that we could not reach him. He would probably return at nightfall to gorge on the flesh of his victims, so we drew lots to decide which of us three is to stalk him and avenge our horses. The lot fell to me.

A little before five o'clock I left the camp, shouldering my express rifle loaded with explosive bullets, taking with me only one of the younger porters, who was armed with a couple of lances. On reaching the banks of the river, where the carcases of our two horses were lying amidst the reeds, I posted myself in a tree which commanded the place where the carcase of the first horse lay. I established myself astride of a large bough, while my "boy" perched himself a little above me.

Before nightfall, while waiting for the lion, I ran through a very old number of the *Journal de Genève*, which I had not found time to read before, at the same time keeping my eyes and ears open. The twilight deepened little by little; the first star shone. The deep silence was broken only by the chirping of insects, sounding like that of crickets or grasshoppers. The night grew darker and darker, and my "boy" sighed deeply on his perch. After several hours of futile waiting I descended from my post, for the lion had not appeared; but not without hearing the dismal cries of hyenas and the yelping of jackals, who had gathered at this improvised feast, grinding the bones of the unhappy companions of our good and evil days. Never had I seen a longer stride than that of my "boy," returning safe and sound to the camp!

July 18th.—Last night the hyenas and jackals were furious, and woke us several times. This morning nothing was left of the carcase of the lioness. We confide our bridles and saddles to some natives, who are to carry them to Kazungula, and then—*en route!* Henceforth walking will be our only mode of travel, for we have only one horse left. We passed through more or less scattered thickets, interspersed with tall trees, bordering the river; we saw numerous spoor of lions and fresh traces of buffalo. This time we pitched our tent near the bank. We were finishing our meal when we heard the grunting of a hippopotamus. Taking our guns, we were soon near the noisy brute, which was snorting and sputtering loudly. It was impossible for us to see him; it was far too dark.

At supper we ate zebra, a meat not so despicable as one might imagine.

July 19th.—We were obliged to cut short the sufferings of our last horse; there was no hope for poor "Tommy," who had been bitten by the murderous tsetse fly, which causes the death of almost all domestic animals in a longer or shorter time. Horses and oxen, once bitten, die rapidly, while donkeys may live for months.' One very curious fact is that the tsetse is found more especially in tracts frequented by buffalos, which do not seem to be affected by its bite.

On such an expedition as ours one must be prepared in advance for all kinds of unforeseen accidents. We are getting on. One more porter has run off to-day.

On several occasions we have seen great veldt fires, which at night are magnificent. These fires destroy a host of insects. The vegetation is so vigorous that the

---

Animals which resist the venom of the tsetse fly are in a very great minority; they are spoken of as being "salted," and fetch very high prices. *Author.*

grass soon pushes up again on the calcined spaces; even the trees do not perish in any great number.

The variety of ants is great: twice already in the space of a few hours our baggage has been attacked by termites.

While out hunting I came across a colony of monkeys with grey-brown fur and blackish muzzles; I do not know their name.

July 20th.—The aspect of the landscape is continually changing. In the neighbourhood where we found ourselves to-day the river flows at the bottom of a valley overlooked by low hills whose crests only are crowned with trees. A decided bend makes it flow from the north, and then the country opens out again, especially on the right bank. In the distance we made out a series of low wooded hills; there I had the good luck again to kill a reedbuck (*Cervicapra arundinacea*), and Reid killed an oribi (*Nanotragus scoparius*), one of the smallest antelopes known.

July 21st. A troop of gnus, taking it into their heads to advance too close to our camp, had to suffer the disastrous consequences of their curiosity; we have stocked our larder extensively. Here we remarked great black ants with flat heads armed with pincers, which they knew how to use at our expense.

July 23rd.—We forded two affluents of the Machili which were not marked on our charts. The natives call them Kanimba and Kamakava. My ammunition fell into the water on this occasion; happily no great harm was done.

We passed several huts made of thatch and surrounded by a high palisade, probably out of fear of wild beasts.

Near by I discovered a native blacksmith. He was

making what appeared to be a hatchet; a large stone
served as anvil, and his assistant blew the fire with a
more than rudimentary bellows. There should, therefore,
be iron ore in this country.

Here, further on, was a vast plantation of water-melons
and gourds. A woman was in the act of cutting them
into little quarters, which she was drying in the sun.

We have among our porters only two Barotsi of the

MATOTELA SMITHS
From a photograph by the Author

reigning tribe; the other belong to subjected tribes –
Matotela, Batoka, &c. We have even one Mashukulumbwe (north-east); he is deprived of his four central
incisive and the lateral superior teeth. According to
custom, a young man of this region may not dream of
taking a wife unless he first of all undergoes this opera-

tion; for, so say the Mashukulumbwe, these teeth resemble those of the zebra.

The camping ground being reached, each group establishes itself apart from the others, so that at night our tent is surrounded by six or seven camp fires; notwithstanding which the "boys" pay mutual visits to laugh and chat. In the firelight they recount the deeds and incidents of the day, with many interjections and exclamations; they imitate the cries of animals to perfection. It is at this time that they like to indulge in the native tobacco, which is so strong as to draw tears from their eyes. It causes maladies of the eye; small-pox also has often trying consequences of the same kind.

They then prepare their meal; this, when the hunting is good, consists of meat, which they simply grill on the burning embers; or, according to circumstances, it may be sorghum, maize, millet, or ground nuts, of which they are extremely fond.*

I observe one of our men making music after his kind; his primitive instrument consists of a grooved tablet of wood, which he rubs with another piece of wood. The sounds he produces are distinct enough, but in no way harmonious.

If, from a physical point of view, the native types vary greatly, the same cannot be said of their garments, which consist chiefly of a loin-cloth fastened to the girdle by a serpent's skin. The more fortunate add the skin of some wild beast, and all are ready to adorn themselves with bracelets, necklaces, earrings, &c. I must not forget one particular, unique of its kind, of the most simplified toilet of a Borotsi: the pocket-handkerchief. This consists of a thin blade of iron, finely wrought, with a handle of the same metal. The whole is perhaps four or five inches

* In the language of the country sorghum = *mabili*; maize = *mpongi*; millet = *matontsa*; ground-nuts = *masambanu*.

MATOPELA VILLAGE AND GRANARIES

Drawn by d'Ostcrop, from a photograph by the Author

long by one or two inches wide, and is hung round the neck by vegetable fibres or tendons. In blowing their noses they use it as a spring, with an extreme dexterity which, I can say from experience, is not a pleasant thing at a camp fire. I may add that these savages have also perfected the manner of blowing the nose which is still

NATIVE POCKET-HANDKERCHIEFS
Sketch by Van Muyden. Author's collection

practised by certain rustic inhabitants of civilised countries.

Nearly all the men are armed with long spears, more or less barbed.

Transactions with the rare natives we meet are effected by means of the ell of white calico (*setsiba*), which is the current money, and by small, white, opaque beads of glass; we bought some eggs just recently with this coin.

On meeting natives we are saluted by the world *lumila*, that is to say, "Good day," or more exactly, "Au revoir." When the natives are armed they lay down their spears at a respectful distance until they are addressed, without ever showing the least signs of impatience. They bring their produce in calabashes hung at the ends of a long staff.

The calabash plays an important part in this country; not only for transporting grain or liquid, but as a utensil.

BOW AND POISONED ARROWS; MANKOYA
Sketch by Van Munden. Author's collection

July 24th.—Along the two banks of the Machili stretch ranges of low hills, leaving a considerable open space between them and the river.

A native whom we encountered gave me a piece of cabbage-palm, white and tender, and very agreeable to eat, which he had just cut.

July 25th-26th.—We camped not far from the affluence of the Wamaroba river, one of the principal tributaries of the Machili on the right bank. We are on the territory of the Mankoya tribe, who are subject to the Barotsi, and we received a visit from a number of them. They sold us sorghum and wild honey, taking beads of white and opaque glass in payment. Several were armed with bows and arrows; some of the latter were poisoned. We enriched our collection with some specimens of these arms.

These Mankoya are of a distinct type. Their abundant coiffure, crinkled and glistening, is astonishing; the

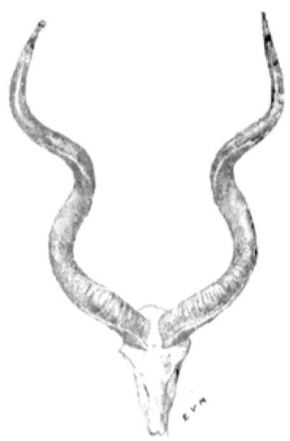

KOODOO, " STREPSICEROS KUDU"
Sketch by Von Magden. Specimen brought home by Author

frequent use of nut-oil, for which they cultivate the plants near their huts, gives their hair a peculiar lustre.

Their teeth are often filed to a sharp point. Some of the Mankoya have a moustache, and even a beard; a rare thing among negroes.

For the first time we encountered natives who made use of cowrie shells as ornaments. This proves that the Portuguese half-castes come here; the people of the country call them *mombari*. The Mankoya have no cattle, not even goats and sheep; they live by the chase.

Our men caught an iguana, and ate the eggs eagerly.

As the asses retarded our march onward, we decided, after considering the matter, to leave them at this place under the care of Moklu, a Bechuana in whom we put confidence, and several men.

WATERBUCK, "COBUS ELLIPSIPRYMNUS."
Sketch by Van Maydeu. Specimen brought home by Author.

Our men will have no lack of food, for in the last three days we have killed several antelopes, all of large size; amongst them the black antelope (*Hippotragus niger*), the koodoo (*Strepsiceros kudu*), whose fine spiral horns were over three feet long; the waterbuck (*Cobus ellipsiprymnus*), a beast of a majestic carriage and almost perfect proportions; and the bubale (*Alcephalus lichtensteinii*), whose elongated head to some extent recalls the zebra's; the two latter fell to my gun. Part of the meat has been smoke-dried, and there will be *biltong* for many days.

Even in places where big game is very abundant we must, as a general thing, undergo great trouble and fatigue to approach it.

July 27th.—North-easterly direction. To cut off an elbow of the Machili we crossed a range of hills and halted near a watercourse called by the natives Sitapo, which does not figure on any map. There were some deserted huts here, and in their midst a tumulus, covered with thatch and surrounded by spoils of the chase. We supposed it to be the tomb of a chief, and that the hut had belonged to him. Further on we met a Mankoya who, judging by his numerous following, must be an important personage. We sat down in the grass and engaged in conversation; a handful of tobacco afforded him much satisfaction. Some of his men had the loin-cloth fastened round the waist by broad girdles of leather artistically wrought. We had numerous visitors in the camp, in particular two drummers, who were responsible for more noise than music, striking their strangely shaped instruments with the fingers and the palms of the hands alternately.

Every day we came across the snares set by the natives to capture guinea-fowl, conies, and other small animals. They are very ingenious. On the path followed by the game a hole is dug, above which is placed a running noose held by a rod bent in tension. When the noose is touched the animal is trapped, or killed by a skilfully adjusted piece of wood.

We also find great pits, often covered with branches, in

which large game is sometimes taken, and these we have carefully to avoid.

July 28th.—We continued crossing the hills. We saw a very dangerous serpent, which Klass Africa warned us not to approach.

At midday we camped again on the banks of the Machili.

July 30th.—After a day's rest we resumed our march. Four Mankoya entered our service for a time. We came to a marsh, which at this season is partly dry; it is cut up by pools and fenny places which are often treacherously hidden by dense rushes; on the right bank is an affluent named Kakoma by the natives. Then, to our relief, the landscape changed for the better; dales with wooded slopes of graceful curves made lines not devoid of grandeur along the wide horizon.

To-day we had the beginning of a mutiny among the porters. The ringleader, Mobana, was summoned before us, and as, after a severe cross-questioning, he was unable to justify his conduct, he had to be severely punished. The calico received by him on account of wages was accordingly withdrawn and burnt on the spot, in the sight of all his comrades, who were also told that those who did not wish to hold to their contracts had only to take themselves off immediately. Not one stirred.

It has been terribly hot to-day.

July 31st.—It was cold last night, with a white frost. The character of the country makes us look forward to reaching our destination. We were mounting rapidly higher above the sea-level; the watercourses on the two banks diminished in importance, the marshes became rarer and rarer, and the depression formed by the river bed grew less and less, until in the course of the day we came to a meadow-land sprinkled with knots of trees, where all trace of the river disappeared. We were at the source, properly so called, which is formed by two distinct branches, both dried up at this season of the year. The aspect of the surrounding country indicates that the Machili must receive a considerable volume of water during the rainy season.

We are on the line of the watershed dividing the waters of those rivers joining the Zambezi on the south from those which, flowing towards the north-east, discharge themselves into the Kafukwe river; the latter joins the Zambezi two hundred miles or more further east. The position of the source of the Machili had not up to the present, to our knowledge, been reckoned by any European.

We are all three in excellent health, and the more pleased at the success of our expedition in that Reid, on two previous expeditions in Africa, was arrested a first time by the wholesale desertion of his porters, and the second time struck down by fever, being three days unconscious and very near to death.

Reid is provided with excellent instruments, and has taken *en route* a number of observations of the latitude of important points. Many times I have had the privilege of assisting him in his work by reading the chronometer, when, armed with the sextant, he has been taking the altitude of a star in the splendid tropical nights, or observing an occultation by means of a powerful telescope. One of the latter observations gave us a reading of $16° 8' 8''$ south latitude; the source of the Machili itself was found to be $16° 9'$ south latitude, at an elevation above sea-level of 3,900 to 3,930 feet.'

    For further technical details of this part of the exploration see the second Appendix. *Author*.

REID TAKING AN OBSERVATION. *Drawn by Van. Hayden*

Reid considers that the task he has undertaken is in great part completed; he will accordingly return more or less directly to the neighbourhood of Kazungula, accompanied by Pirie, hunting the while, and we shall meet later on at Kazungula.

As for me, I have decided to cross the Borotsi country in a north-westerly direction as far as Lealuyi; the capital, and the residence of King Lewanika and M. Coillard, the celebrated missionary; thence I shall descend the Zambezi by canoe as far as Kazungula, and also visit the missionary stations. Nineteen native porters are put at my disposal, and I shall take in addition Klass Africa, the Hottentot elephant-hunter already mentioned, accompanied by his servants; I shall also have Watcher and Kudumann, both Bechuanas.

In addition to the necessary provisions, arms, ammunition, tent, and utensils, I am taking with me as the medium of exchange, or as presents for the chiefs, some hundred and sixty yards of white calico, twenty-five pounds of beads of various colours, twenty-four blankets, six dozen handkerchiefs of lively colours, knives, thread, &c. The loads are divided amongst the men, and all is ready for departure.

CHAPTER VII

ACROSS THE KINGDOM OF THE BAROTSI

Across the kingdom of the Barotsi to Lealuyi—The Njoko river, in the Matotela country—The Lumbi river—The Lui river, in the Mokwenga country—Sefula.

August 1st.—A hard white frost last night, and a heavy dew this morning. Our last meal together; I shook hands with Reid and Pirie, and set out at the head of my twenty-five men—a number which will vary more or less according to circumstances. In the evening I encamped on the banks of the Kakoma river, an affluent of the right bank of the Machili.

Henceforth the direction taken will be approximately north-west.

Next morning I crossed the Wamaroba, an affluent of the right bank of the Machili. At present it forms a marsh, which caused us some difficulty, wetting us to the knees in mire. Before reaching this river we crossed a hill, on which we found fresh spoor of eland (*Oreas canna*), which I followed with several men; unfortunately the wind was unfavourable.

The afternoon march led us to the valley through which the Kamitwe river should flow, a marshy stream which did not inconvenience us so much as that we crossed this morning.

We then found another watercourse, the Kamanga,

which probably joins the Njoko; the direction is south-east. After climbing our sixth hill to-day we found ourselves in the basin of the Njoko, and at nightfall the camp was pitched on the slope of a valley which confines the bed of the Mania, an affluent of the left bank of the Njoko. During these two first days we met with no human beings, nor with any habitation; the large game which ought to be found in such districts at this season is extremely rare. After to-day's hard marching the men were forced to stretch themselves by the fires without having eaten first.

As usual, great heat during the day.

COMB OF CARVED WOOD FROM THE BANKS OF THE NJOKO
Sketch by Van Muyden
Author's collection

August 3rd.—We followed the course of the Mania and arrived at a collection of huts called Meori; these villages are known by the names of their chiefs. My men were delighted at the sight. They hurried their pace and began to think of the provisions they would find in the bulging calabashes that I should have emptied before them. But what patience is necessary! We were only at the beginning of the day, and not until two o'clock was it possible to make a generous allowance of food. In the first place, the chief has to be warned of my intention of holding a market, and the news is spread among the inhabitants, who, according to whether they are or are not so disposed, go in search of the necessary provisions, which often have still to be prepared. At last men and women arrive one by one, and squat down at a distance, motionless. Little by little they set before me the vessels —wooden platters or calabashes—in which they bring sorghum and ground-nuts. Some want to be paid in blue glass beads, some in white, and they are far from being always easily contented.

We crossed the limit separating the Mankoya from the Matotela tribe. To this day the latter tribe visit their neighbours the Mankoya to exchange spades against slaves. Seven spades are usually considered as the equivalent of a human being! For the morrow, a day of rest, the camp was pitched on the left bank of the Njoko, below the confluence of the Mania, amid superb *motsauli* or *massivi* trees—a tree of majestic shape and deep green foliage, reminding one of the oak. This tree bears a red fruit, shaped like a flat bean, much appreciated by the natives.

PILLOW OF CARVED WOOD FROM THE BANKS OF THE NJOKO
Sketch by Mme Magden
Author's collection

August 4th.—This valley of the Njoko forms a charming landscape, surrounded by wooded hills, on whose flanks the numerous villages stand out as large brown spots. Near the villages large spaces cleared by burning indicate their plantations. To establish a plantation the negroes begin by rooting up the grass and burning it in heaps; they then work the soil.

On approaching one sees on every side the trunks of trees with calcined branches remaining in the midst of these cultivated lands.

We have quite a rush of visitors, who offer us sorghum

flour and curdled milk; the latter they call *mafi*. Meat we have to do without, as the natives bring into camp nothing but consumptive fowls, stale eggs, and fleshless goats. Several of these natives find themselves able to

A WAR SPEAR, A HUNTING SPEAR, AND A FISH SPEAR
Sketch by Van Muyden. Author's collection

spend several hours in musing about the camp. Decidedly time has not the same value for them as for us. Very observant, they have a great mobility of expression, and a laugh comes readily to their lips. I am astonished, in many among them, to meet with traits which, save for the black skin, recall the Jewish type. The Matotela often pull out the two central upper incisors.

Here are beside me men whose every tuft of hair is

A MATOTELA TYPE
From a photograph by the Author

terminated by a regular cone of brown paste, made of crushed earth-nuts. It is their method of making the hair jut out: the preparation of this coiffure requires two days, and ought to last several weeks. Sacrificing their ease to their vanity, the natives use as a pillow a little wooden trestle like that of the Japanese. Their costume is simplified to the simplest; for arms many of them carry, in addition to the barbed lance, a finer and more pointed spear, which serves for taking fish. I was able to obtain some of them in exchange for some large, clear blue beads, which are in great demand.

This afternoon I visit the dwelling of the chief Sibupa. An enclosure, formed by trunks of trees two or three yards in height, contains a large central hut surrounded by eleven smaller ones—all of them round, built of reeds, and covered with thatch. A long tapering drum hangs on a tree close to a bundle of spears.

Outside the entrance a roof shelters a blacksmith's establishment, facing which are the granaries, small buildings elevated from the ground, making one think of huge beehives. A woman is bruising sorghum in a great wooden bowl.

Further on, by the waterside, are the cattle, of two different breeds; the small, muscular cows with smooth hair and short horns belong to the Moshukulumbwe breed; the others, which are far more powerful, belong to the Borotsi properly so called. Many of these beasts have the ears artificially shaped.

At nightfall I hear the deafening sound of a kind of elongated drum covered with skin, which music announces a dance for the night to the group of huts neighbouring. Knowing that in a savage country these affairs are a cause of disorder, and wishing to keep my men in hand, I forbade them to go to the dance, warning them that I should make rounds in person during the evening, and that those who did not answer to their names need no longer consider themselves in my service. The aforesaid muster

was called at an unexpected time—every one was present. These negroes must be treated as veritable children—that is to say with justice, but also with great firmness, otherwise desertion would soon begin.

August 5th.—We crossed to the right bank of the Njoko, the water scarcely reaching our knees. During the rainy season the Njoko is navigable to the Zambezi.

The neighbouring population came to assist our crossing, as well as the two chiefs Manimbula and Maoya; the latter was more extensively clothed than the generality of his subjects, a flannel shirt covering his shoulders.

We met with a herd being driven swiftly to pasture by black shepherds, armed with spears and with plumes on their heads, drawing joyful sounds from their pipes.

I visited a chief named Surukurukuru, living not far from here; while waiting for him to return from the forest we seated ourselves near the granaries, and there perceived three great rolls of sorghum, cleverly laced with creepers, hanging from poles. These were the tribute for King Lewanika. At last came Surukurukuru himself, an old man, escorted by three younger men. He gave us a guide.

In the afternoon we marched through a forest of lofty trees. We then forded the Kambona river without suffering much inconvenience from the liquid mire of its banks, and encamped beside it. The Kambona is a tributary on the right bank of the Njoko.

According to our custom, as soon as we arrive at the chosen camping-place, each man has his task; these are responsible for the tent, which they have to learn to pitch rapidly; others go off to mow down withered grasses, which are spread on the ground, to cut wood, and search for water. Soon we have great fires burning. The men

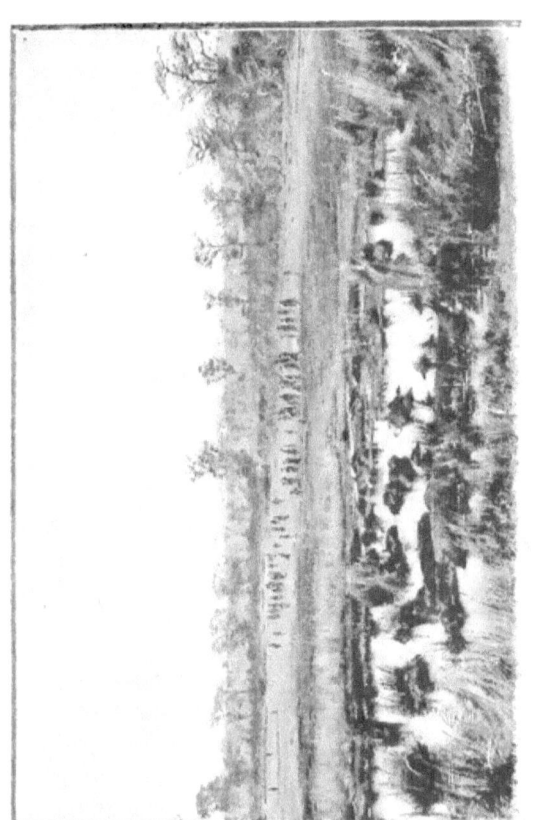

NATIVES TOBOGGING THE NJOKO

Drawn by Isombier, from a photograph by the Author

like to group themselves by tribes; there are accordingly five or six groups. Now comes the time for distributing food; one man in each group is appointed to receive it.

Then all are busy cooking and eating. After the meal conversation begins again, and, as I have mentioned before, they tell over again the incidents of the day.

THE CHIEF SUSI KURI KURU
From a photograph by the Author

Little by little they stretch themselves out by the fire, some of them not possessing even a skin to protect their almost entirely naked bodies from the cold, and they draw so close to the embers that many of them carry traces of severe burns.

Two or three of them possess a musical instrument called *kangombio*; there are ten notes, made of slips of

iron of unequal lengths, which are fixed on a thin strip of
wood resting in its turn upon a hollow calabash. With
this instrument they accompany very soft and melancholy
melodies which often continue late into the night. The
fires are fed during the night, and if I wake I am still
almost sure to hear whisperings here and there.

The porter Lipone and one of his comrades are down
with fever; I am treating them with strong doses of
quinine. They are incapable of carrying their loads, and
to-day I have a chance to engage two new men. One of
them, Litaba, has for his travelling equipment, besides
the usual loin-cloth, a sort of kerchief woven of palm-fibre.

August 6th.—We reached an enchanting little lake,
about 500 yards long, with azure waters, surrounded
with verdure. I gave it the name of "Blue Water."
From this lake the river Ikwe, an affluent of the right
bank of the Njoko, should take its source. The landscape, except for the absence of firs, reminds one of
certain parts of the Jura. I think I am not claiming
too much for myself when I say that this lake does not
yet figure on any geographical chart.

After having been deprived of meat for several days, I
was greatly appreciating a guinea-hen killed yesterday
evening, when there arrived on the part of the chief
Surukurukuru, a man of foresight, a second guide as
travelling companion to the first; his name is Damusiba.
His hair, interwoven with vegetable fibres, forms an
infinity of little tresses, while his comrade has the crown
of his head modestly adorned with a tuft of feathers.

Accompanied by these new recruits, we skirted a long
hill and entered the valley of the Kwemba, another
affluent of the right bank of the Njoko. After having
plunged through a quaking, spongy bog and experiencing
the disagreeable sensation that it would be possible to

disappear there entirely, we thought we should easily be able to cross the Kwemba. We were mistaken; the water reached our shoulders.

On reaching the other bank, I had to oversee the business of fording, and to send help to the weaker or more timid ones. Several of the loads, which had to be carried on the head, ran considerable risks; above all the case containing my photographic plates. With patience, however, all passed without accident.

August 7th.—It was cold last night. At 6.30 this morning the thermometer marked only 37·3° Fahr.

The tent, as usual, has to be rapidly folded up. The loads, which are placed in order beside it every night, are put together and taken up by their respective porters, always the same. At this moment the sick men have to report themselves at the tent. After a light meal the more than primitive utensils and vessels are washed, and we are ready to resume the march. According to circumstances, I take either the head or the tail of the column. Klass Africa is my interpreter for transmitting orders; he tells me he has often had difficulty in understanding such and such of the men, so much do the dialects spoken vary. The men, it is true, belong to different tribes; besides Klass Africa, who is a Hottentot, and Watcher and Kudumann, who are Bechuanas, there are Barotsi, Batoka, Matotela, Mashukulumbwe, Mambunda, and Mankoya. They vary in type as well as in dialect.

While marching I have two men specially attached to my service. Picaninny, a Morotsi, a sturdy fellow, carries my spare guns and my cartridges. Besides wearing the skin of some wild beast fastened over his shoulders, he sports a long pointed hat ornamented on either side by two still longer feathers. Then there is Sibette, a quick,

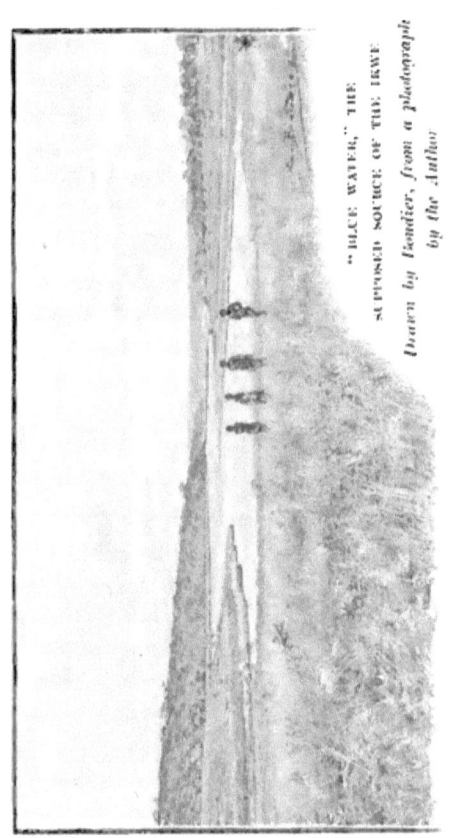

"BLUE WATER," THE SUPPOSED SOURCE OF THE IKWE

Drawn by Eardley, from a photograph by the Author

intelligent boy, always gay and contented, who as a rule does not trouble himself with either skin or hat; a piece of cotton-stuff bound round the waist by a serpent-skin is sufficient for him. Moshukulumbwe by birth, he was carried off from his native country in a raid while quite young. He is responsible for my photographic apparatus,

SIPULULU
From a photograph by the Author

which is still intact, in spite of all our ups and downs. This fortunate result is due largely to the obliging assistance of the Director of the "Comptoir Suisse de Photographie" at Geneva, who had the apparatus and plates packed in a very ingenious manner. The camera, 9 × 12 cm., is a perfect instrument of exploration—light,

About 3½ in. × 4¾ in.

solid, simple, and practical in use. It occupies very little space.

This morning we had another long hill to cross. It led us to the valley of the Njonjo, probably an affluent on the left bank of the Lumbi river. In our present situation, and in the dry season, it may be ten or twelve

CROSSING THE NJOKO
From a photograph by the Author

yards wide—fine clear water, deep, and swiftly running. Impossible to ford it; happily we found some branches bound together by creepers, forming a shaky bridge; we had to cross it with every care. One by one all the packages arrived the other side without mishap.

During the first halt of the day I was finishing a more than frugal meal, when one of the Mankoya, usually skilful in searching for it, brought in an unexpected addition—a delicious comb of wild honey. He had followed up a *skesson Cuculus indicator*), an intelligent bird which draws the attention of the traveller by its cries. It flies about near him, and if it is followed leads him to the place where the honey is to be found. His conduct is not altogether disinterested, for, the comb once taken from the tree, he regales himself on the larvae and *débris*. The natives look for honey with great willingness.

Six of the men arrived two hours late; as they could not justify themselves, and were vigorous fellows, they had to take the head of the column under my supervision when we resumed our march.

During the afternoon's march we had another interminable hill to climb, at the foot of which we found the Kaponi, at present dry. In the rainy season it probably joins the Njonjo, crossed this morning.

Here are the names given by the natives to some of the numerous species of trees which more or less intermittently people the forests: the majestic *motsouli* or *massiri*, whose wood is extremely hard, has already been named. The *mobula* recalls the maple or yoke-elm; its wood is good for joiners' work, and it bears an edible stone-fruit. The *motondo* has a light foliage; its wood is straight in grain, and used for making the handles of spades, axes, &c. The *mokou*, less ornamental than the preceding, does not bear fruit; the natives use it for making oars and domestic utensils. Then comes the *majongolo*, which is useful for making spoons; it has an edible fruit. There are numbers of *moholuholu* trees, a shrub something like a small plum-tree, bearing large round fruits with a hard rind, which the natives eat in great quantity, but which the European should avoid for fear of dysentery.

The system employed this morning answered well. In spite of a long march and extreme heat there were no stragglers, and we reached our proposed halting-place.

August 8th.—Last night the termites began to attack one of the rugs left in the tent.

During the middle of the day we crossed the swamp formed by the Masetti, not far from its confluence with the Lumbi river; the latter flows through the midst of a wide valley, which at this point is not so charming as that of the Njoko, but the lines of the horizon are grander.

The natives here have an ingenious manner of making gardens, or rather plantations, which are visibly raised; a trench is left all round by the earth taken out to form the surface.

We entered the village of the chief Mayumba, where we found it necessary to hold a market to obtain provisions. The chief was not long in making his appearance, escorted by ten of his subjects. He did not seem to be the personification of candour. After the usual salutation he commenced by telling me that corn was very scarce, and that he could not let me have any. However, it was imperative to obtain it, for I had thirty hungry men behind me, and nothing but one calabash of groundnuts. We could do no more than be patient. Seating myself under a tree, I had the bag brought me containing the glass beads, and then, as usual on such occasions, I exhibited my necklaces, white, blue, and black. The circle closed in; my objects of exchange were discussed—a good sign; finally I heard the sound of women bruising sorghum. The replenishing of our stores was assured. Mayumba himself disappeared, returning with a black kid, borne on the shoulders of one of his followers. This he gave me as a personal present; a knife was immediately offered in return. In a short time I had more food in front of me than my men could carry.

I visited the chief's dwelling. For the first time in this country I saw huts with earthen walls. Near by some children were playing, their stomachs protuberant through improper diet.

Mayumba, for the time, was full of consideration. But, knowing from experience that it doesn't do to have one's camp near a village, I decided to cross to the other bank of the Lanubi this afternoon.

We saw in this neighbourhood the trail followed by the missionaries of the Zambezi when they go by land from Kazungula to Lealuyi—a trail that we shall frequently cross in the future. Mayumba himself acted as our guide. We floundered about for a long time in a miry swamp before reaching the actual river, which we crossed easily, thanks to the two canoes of a boatman brought by the chief.

Klass Africa is suffering this evening from fever, caused by frequent passage through water and swamps during the latter part of our journey. This circumstance prevents me from pursuing the gnus sighted in the neighbourhood, and obliges me to keep a close watch on the men.

August 9th.—We were unable to advance: Klass Africa was very ill to-day. I am giving him strong doses of quinine and calomel. He passed the day stretched out in a state of torpor, semi-unconscious, and scarcely able to move.

Klass Africa's illness, in forcing me to halt, puts me in a very difficult and disquieting position. When these natives are not working they easily get demoralised, and in such a case desertion *en masse* is to be feared, which puts an end to an expedition. Besides this, I reckon that at the rate at which my thirty men are making the provisions disappear, and notwithstanding the food bought yesterday at Mayumba, we have nourishment for forty-eight hours only—two calabashes of sorghum, two of beans, and one of ground-nuts. At my bidding one of my men, Mabona, swims across the Lumbi to solicit

MABONA AND THE MOHOLI HOLO TREE
From a photograph by the Author

another interview from Mayumba, but the chief shows no intention of responding to my invitation.

Three of the porters deserted this morning, and I let them go. I am not sorry to be rid of Mabenga and Libwe, with whom I was far from satisfied. As for the third, the quiet and gentle little Lipone, he was too weak for his task. For several days he had merely followed the caravan, and his load had been divided among his comrades.

For these reasons I did not leave the camp until a little before sunset, when I tried to surprise some of the antelopes that frequent the borders of the marsh dechwe, *Cobus lechê*). How welcome fresh meat would be!

I was not long before I sunk up to the knees in the spongy ground, and was almost within range of a group of antelopes taking their rest, when I was suddenly brought up by an angle of the river, at this part impassable. On my return I learned that another of the porters, Jacob, and the two guides given me by Surukurukuru, had profited by my short absence by deserting. After all, I am as glad to lose Jacob as I was to lose Mabenga and Libwe. I was obliged to reprimand them severely on many occasions, and the disappearance of these undisciplined fellows will, I trust, conduce to the order of the caravan. As for my guides, they were probably homesick, and we shall have to do without their help. Nevertheless, my position is nothing less than enviable!

August 10th.—At six o'clock this morning a thermometer placed on a case in front of my tent indicated 34° F. Yesterday afternoon, in the same place but exposed to the sun, it marked 109° F.

There was a little improvement in Klass Africa's condition. After a serious conversation with him—since he will not consent to go south by himself with a few men, as I proposed he should—I made him understand the urgency of going forward, for we shall not be able to revictual for two or three days. After yesterday's desertions the loads are divided afresh, and I find that at

MARKET AT MANYUEMA
From a photograph by the Author

present I have precisely the necessary number of men. We form, all told, a column of twenty-three men.

During the day the nature of the country changed; the hills were further apart and also more elongated, forming plateaux. Near the little Musana pool we saw the spoor of elephants. Arriving at the Kambai lake I bade the men fill their calabashes at its blue waters, for we shall find no water to-night. In Africa it is important to arrange one's halts where the indispensable liquid is likely to be found. The men suffer from its privation more than from that of food.

After crossing a wooded plain we camped under a fine *motsaoli*. Klass is suffering greatly again this evening. He cannot take quinine any longer, as it causes nervous trouble, so I have followed the advice given me before my departure, trying friction with sulphate of quinine in powder under the armpits, while fortifying him with the most nutritious food I have.

August 11th.—The sulphate of quinine has produced a good effect, and we are able to continue the march—alternations of wide plains and wooded tracts. We sight two small lakes, and pass the night not far from the second.

August 12th.—The thermometer sank to freezing point at six o'clock this morning, while the heat made itself felt during the day strongly as usual. These great differences of temperature, which succeed one another with an equally great rapidity, are not exactly good for the health.

The character of the country is the same as yesterday; for the rest, there was sand, very tiring to walk on. We found fresh water in a well, just before undertaking a wide plain covered with ant-hills as hard as rock.

CROSSING THE MARSH. *Drawn by Van Muyden*

At midday I reached the border of the Motondo river, where I waited for my men, who came up one by one. Two Mankoya, Gonena and Malia, made me lose the afternoon. They did not turn up until after five o'clock in the evening, and as one of them carried some things indispensable for cooking my meal was not ready until six.

First of all the two culprits have to appear before me. It is essential, in order to attain the desired end, to reprimand all attempts at disorder with justice and firm-

DRINKING CALABASH AND SPOONS
Sketch by Van Muyden. Author's collection

ness. The men are assembled, and informed that the conduct of their two comrades will prevent us all from reaching the village to-day, where we should have found abundance of food.

I having heard their bad excuses, the two Mankoya will make their camp fire apart from the others to-night, and will not be included in the distribution of what grain remains.

Then, march! The sun is already low on the horizon,

HMLY:
From a photograph by the Author

the twilight deepens rapidly, and we have just time to cross to the right bank of the Motondo, an affluent of the Lui, before night. To-morrow morning on our departure the water would be too cold. We are soon trampling through the marshy plants, and then plunge into the mud, and into swamps where the water ends by reaching our waists. The whole river is perhaps seven or eight hundred yards wide. Once across, the great camp-fires which are quickly burning are regarded, as every one will easily understand, with entire satisfaction. The last calabash of ground-nuts is divided among the men.

August 13th.—We reached at an early hour the valley of the Lui river. Here once more we had to plunge into slippery, viscous mud, and cross pools where the water reached the knee. Near the deep river we perceived with pleasure a native running from the neighbouring village; for a handful of white beads he took us over one by one to the opposite bank in a dug-out canoe.

One of the porters, a Moshukulumbwe by birth, profited by this occasion of a moment's rest to make a fire after his fashion. He held a long and very hard stick, which finally wore away like a pencil, to a small piece of very dry wood, making the former rotate vigorously between his hands, while keeping round it some dry vegetable fibres, which were not long in catching fire. The second operation consisted in putting a little tobacco in a reed. He closed one extremity of the reed with grass, and then, from this improvised pipe, drew with delight two or three whiffs of smoke, and passed the instrument to his particular friends, who followed his example.

On the whole, these men do not smoke much; they prefer taking snuff, made of tobacco, cultivated and prepared in the country. It plays a great part in their existence. When they meet any one of their acquaintance

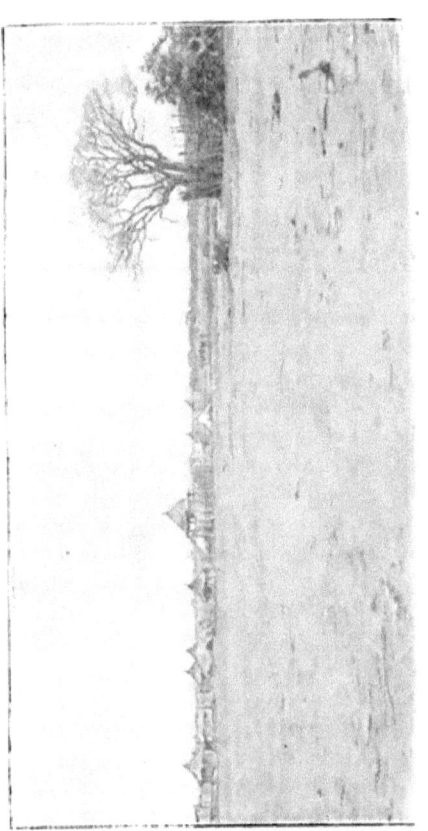

A LANDSCAPE IN DAHOMEY

Drawn by Cavalier, from a photograph by the Author

while travelling, after squatting down and clapping hands according to custom, they offer one another snuff, which they carry in a little gourd suspended at the waist; they sprinkle it in the palms of their hands, and each one takes a pinch.

I may mention here that the salutations of the natives of these parts, often very bizarre, vary infinitely, according to the position of the individual and his degree of relationship to the man he is saluting. For instance, I have been unable to repress a smile on seeing one of my men spit amiably on the shoulder of a traveller he chanced to meet: a sign of friendship which would certainly be little appreciated in Europe.

We are on the territory of the Makwenga people, who own cattle and work in iron.

Here we are established under a superb *motsouli*; but I can give my men nothing to eat! I have nothing left. Picaninny has been sent twice to the neighbouring village to inform the inhabitants that we wish to buy provisions. The time passes, but nothing arrives; the delay is even greater than usual. It appears that in this part of the country the inhabitants keep their provisions at some distance in the country, and not near their huts, for fear of pillage. At last a file of men and women become visible on the veldt, carrying calabashes and large wooden dishes. They arrive with the chief Moamanomne at their head. This time the small opaque beads are in request. They bring us curdled milk, sorghum, and sweet potatoes, Moamanomne offering me a basket of the latter as a present, and seeming satisfied to receive in turn a European article.

A generous allowance of sweet potatoes is served out to the men, and the sorghum is kept in reserve. We now march until nightfall.

August 14th.—A long sandy hill; paroquets flying from branch to branch. At the morning halt Klass Africa arrived late, he had a fresh and violent access of fever, and was as weak as a child; you could have knocked him down with a feather. He had to be covered up in his blanket, and given a stimulant, but in spite of all he fell into a state of stupor.

MY MEN IN THE GREAT LOKOTSI PLAIN
Drawn by Boudier, from a photograph by the Author

Not until four o'clock were we able to resume our march across the wide plain, at the other side of which the village of Shiribero could be seen. There I was able to obtain a few fowls, which were caught under my eyes by children, who were delighted with their task. We pitched camp not far from Nanjekua lake. Klass Africa was at the end of his strength; I must begin the sulphate of quinine frictions again.

August 15*th.* The rubbings with sulphate of quinine are a decided success with Klass; this morning he was very much better, and we were able to start at the usual time.

The country is becoming more and more thickly populated; in the morning we passed a village where we obtained abundance of dried sweet potatoes and manioc in exchange for white beads. Near by I saw a native carving, out of a block of *mokoa* wood, a *tubana*, or milk-jar, with the most primitive sort of tool. He had just put the finishing touches to one jar, and gave it me in exchange for a red kerchief. Here there were many head of cattle.

When once our meal was finished (boiled sweet potatoes and curdled milk), we resumed our march, leaving on the west a plain on which were grouped the round huts of several large villages. The women were labouring in the open, using short-handled hoes, bent double at their work. Several of them carried children slung in skins at their backs, so that one saw nothing but the heads of the little niggers. We finished the day by climbing, in an intense heat, a long, sandy hill, very trying to march on, and encamped near the Ikulwei lake.

August 16*th.*—On setting out we had to climb another hill, more or less tree-clad, on which I killed two guinea-fowl. During the morning we came to the valley of the Sefula, through which runs the river of the same name. Many villages, and great activity in the fields. M. Coillard, the missionary, in teaching the natives to drain the waters of this valley, has put a great deal of land in cultivation.

At midday we arrived at the missionary station of Sefula itself, built on the summit of a hillock. It was

THE CHURCH AT LEALUI.
From a photograph by the Author.

founded by M. Coillard in 1886, and here is the tomb of Mme Coillard, the faithful and intrepid companion of this heroic missionary. This station will be occupied by M. Davit, recently from Europe, whom we had the pleasure of meeting at Palapye. M. Coillard has continued his march forward; he is now at Lealuyi, the capital of the Borotsi country, and the residence of King Lewanika. He is seconded by M. and Mme Adolphe Jalla.

A saw-mill has been established at Sefula, for the requirements of the mission, and it is here that M. Coillard wishes to found a training-school for native evangelists, as well as an industrial school.

The black evangelists from Basutoland whom we meet at Sefula make everything easy for us.

August 17th.—We rose at a quarter past three. An hour later we were *en route*, and were soon crossing the plain separating Sefula from Lealuyi. It is under water during the rains, for which reason all the villages are built on hillocks. In the second part of our march we crossed the Nebubela river.

This great plain, bordered by chains of hills to the east and west, seems to be the bed of an ancient lake, and is not lacking in sublimity.

At last we perceived the missionary station, the church of which looks like a lighthouse from a distance; the large huts of Lealuyi stood out more and more clearly. This part also of our expedition is successful; one last halt to set all in order, and we reach the missionary station, where I receive from M. Coillard, at present unwell, and from M. and Mme Adolphe Jalla, a welcome which quickly makes me forget my past difficulties.

After finding, with my companions, the source of the Machili—the first object we proposed to ourselves—I have crossed the kingdom of the Barotsi as far as Lealuyi, the residence of King Lewanika, and so my second object has also happily been attained.

Summing up, I may say that this latter journey can be divided into two distinct parts :—

1. The country between the Machili and Lumbi rivers, hitherto unexplored in this latitude, consists of a series of wooded hills, intersected by dales and valleys through which run the affluents of the three rivers, Machili, Njoko, and Lumbi, which on the whole run from north to south in order to empty themselves into the great river.

2. Arrived on the banks of the Lumbi, I approached the Zambezi, which, as may easily be seen by the map, forms a long curve from Kazungula to Lealuyi, and crossed the trail followed by the missionaries, when they travel from one to other of these stations by land.

The nature of the country is different, the contours of the surface are more extended, the rivers are less numerous. One of the most important is the Motondo; another is the Lui; these two unite further to the south before discharging themselves into the Zambezi. Large vleys or lagoons are found here and there in these regions. Several of these, so I am told, communicate with the Zambezi in time of flood, and receive its surplus waters.

CHAPTER VIII

KING LEWANIKA AND THE MISSIONARY, M. COILLARD

At Lealuyi, the capital of King Lewanika—Nalolo, the residence of the Mokwai.

SUNDAY, *August 18th.*—I woke to the cheerful sound of a bell. No long marches, no swamps, to-day! This morning I was present at the Sunday school held in the chapel by Mme Jalla, who teaches ninety to a hundred adults and children, with the help of black evangelists. Excellent discipline and great attention. Later on M. Adolphe Jalla preached the sermon; and although he has not yet decided to become a convert, King Lewanika took his place on the right of the platform. What progress! And it was he who, a few years ago, commanded the throats of seven of his chiefs to be cut in one day!

The congregation numbered 350 to 400, including the prime minister and many of the dignitaries of the kingdom. When the king leaves the chapel his subjects, according to the etiquette of the country, crouch on their hams and slowly clap their hands. The king was at afternoon worship also.

We were eating supper when Lewanika sent me a present of an enormous calabash of curdled milk, and to my hosts a piece of young hippopotamus roasted. This meat, tender and savoury, is like pork when it is cut from a young animal.

August 19th.—To-day (Monday), accompanied by M. Jalla, who was good enough to introduce me, I went into Lealuyi in order to send the king the presents I was charged to offer him in the name of the expedition, and which, according to etiquette, had to be presented before

M. COILLARD
From a photograph by M. Boissonnas, taken in Geneva

the first visit. The presents consisted of a Männlicher cavalry carbine, latest model, with cartridges, blankets, coloured handkerchiefs, and articles of clothing.

We followed the great causeway constructed by M. Coillard, which joins the missionary station and the capital. It is crossed by a wooden bridge under which the canal passes. This causeway is the sole means of communication with Lealuyi in the intervals of the rainy seasons (*mounda*), at which latter times it is necessary to cross the submerged plain by canoe.

We left a group of huts on our right—the king's granaries. We approached and crossed the public place, which is planted with rubber-trees. Here the king himself delivers justice. We arrived at the entrance of his residence, which is surrounded by a high palisade of reeds. This house, situated in the centre of Lealuyi, is separated from the huts of the chiefs and subjects by a wide circular walk.

In this country the oligarchical order is very severe, and the huts vary in size according to the importance of the chiefs. The same holds good in all the relations of life: an inferior, for example, has not the right to have arms or dishes as well decorated as those of his superior in rank.

A narrow opening in the screen of reeds led us into an interior central courtyard. Here is Lewanika's house. Contrary to the custom of the country, it is rectangular, and the walls are made of beaten earth mixed with cow-dung, which takes the place of lime. Eighteen pillars of wood support a pitched roof of thatch. Facing this, on the other side of the court, is the *kushandi*, the king's private chamber. Surrounding the house, properly so called, is the harem of large round huts, thirty feet high and admirably built. Although included in the royal residence, each hut is surrounded by a high palisade. Everything is very neat.

The king is a polygamist. This fact has hitherto kept him from becoming a convert to Christianity, although he fosters the religion in his kingdom, and attends worship with great assiduity.

From the political point of view, each of his wives represents a group of vassals or a tribe.

We were received by Lewanika in a hall carpeted and hung with mats. He made us sit down beside him. A man in the prime of life, tall and stout; his face is shaven, save for a little black beard. He was clad for the occasion in a check suit, holding in his hand, as a fly-killer, a gnu's tail ornamented with glass beads. The expression of his face was extremely mobile.

The presents were placed before him; then, always with the obliging assistance of M. Jalla, I thanked him,

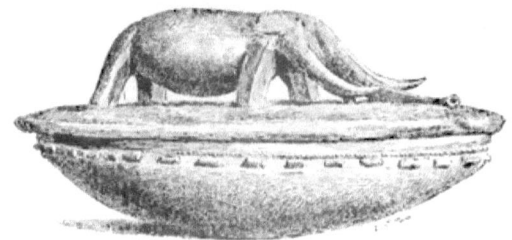

A ROYAL DISH IN CARVED WOOD, GIVEN BY KING LEWANIKA
Sketch by Van Muyden. Author's collection

in the name of the expedition, for having allowed us to enter his territory. He asked me questions on the route followed, told me he was willing to give me, from a geographical point of view, the boundaries of his kingdom. He is going to fix a day for this purpose.

The mechanism of the Männlicher, which I explained, interested him, for he is a hunter. It was the same with the photographic apparatus, which he wished to examine in detail. He gave me permission to photograph him.

We were already some distance from the enclosure when we were rejoined by one of his retainers, who brought us, on the part of the king, two large umbrellas, with which to return to the station ; a pleasing attention, having regard to the intense heat. Of the two men I had brought with me to carry the presents, one, Sibette, was taken with such a fright at the sight of the king that he fled ; the other, Kudumann, awaited us in the most humble of postures.

Lewanika grants free access to his residence to M. Coillard and to M. and Mme Adolphe Jalla. I was privileged to accompany the latter in the missionary

STOOL IN CARVED WOOD, GIVEN BY KING LEWANIKA
Sketch by Van Muyden. Author's collection

circuit which they make regularly at Lealuyi. We went into the dwellings of several of the king's wives, in particular that of the queen Longa, who received us crouching upon her mats in a very low pavilion. She was draped with cotton stuffs of glaring colours; her arms were adorned with superb ivory bracelets. Her servants—or rather slaves, for they are far from being free—were dressing furs for their mistress near the large hut. Longa herself was anxious to do the honours of her residence. All the huts of the harem are the same ; in the centre the principal chamber, carpeted with mats, about sixteen feet high; and round this a circular corridor.

We paid another visit to Katoka, a younger sister of the king; her husband is third in rank in the kingdom. Among her servants Mme Jalla found one of her young pupils engrossed in some needlework—an amusing contrast with her picturesque costume.

It is the custom for the owner of the house to give salutation first, and that only when their visitors are seated, if they have brought seats, or if they have not, crouched upon the ground.

We then entered another interior, that of the princess Mokena. Large black circles were painted round her eyes, standing out against the deep brown of her skin. A black line also crossed her forehead, and divided the nose into two equal parts.

On returning to the missionary station we met on the causeway one of the paddlers of the royal barge, wearing a red kerchief round his head. The honour of propelling the king upon the water is not without its drawbacks. As it is imperative to paddle very quickly, if one of the paddlers shows signs of fatigue he is unceremoniously thrown overboard, when a canoe in the king's retinue picks him up.

August 21st.—The king sent me a fat ox; a fine present, for famine reigns in the neighbourhood, and the locusts have ravaged this part of the kingdom.

Katoka also sent me a large jar of maize.

Almost every day I have the privilege of holding extremely interesting conversations with M. Coillard, although he is suffering greatly, and unable to leave his hut.

August 22nd.—Lewanika has not been long in appointing an afternoon to give me the data required of him. Despite his continual occupations, M. Jalla, with his habitual courtesy, was good enough to accompany me and act once more as interpreter. We found the king in the *kashandi*, which is built after the old-time model of Borotsi dwellings, much in use before the Makololo had invaded the country. The Barotsi, conservatives as they are, continue to build their houses in the old style. The form of this building may be compared to the hull of a boat turned upside down and resting on bastings. Save for the base, the walls of the *kashandi* are built of reeds. To consolidate them large plaits of black and white reeds are employed. A pitched roof, supported by props of wood, completes the structure. Two small low doors, on opposite sides, give access to it.

Lewanika made us sit down, one at his right and one at his left; along the principal wall several dignitaries were squatting on mats—in particular the *Gambella* Scopi, the prime minister, a corpulent personage, whose grizzled head was covered with a coloured cap. He wore no other clothing to-day but a large piece of dark blue cloth rolled round his loins. Round his neck hung a necklet of large blue glass beads, from which depended a *koupa*, a polished shell, which for a long time has represented the value of a slave.

Our charts were spread out in front of Lewanika; the compass interested him. After several questions the king confirmed what I have already said—that to his knowledge, the route I had followed between the Machili and Lumbé rivers had not been explored hitherto in this latitude.

In the latter part of this novel kind of geographical convention, Lewanika gave me some interesting particulars of the frontiers of his kingdom, especially of the very little known northern frontier, which in all probability is

A HUT OF THE ROYAL HAREM
From a photograph by the Author

in the neighbourhood of the watershed dividing the Congo and Zambezi basins, and also of the tribes inhabiting that part, which are still less known. He had called together for the occasion several chiefs or subjects. They squatted in the court apart from us, waiting until they should be called by the king. Then they entered on their knees, bowing very low and clapping their hands, and sat on their heels. Seajika, the king's secretary, sat in front of him and took part in the discussion, as well as the *Gambella Seopi* and others. As I have said, Lewanika gave me

WOODEN LUBANA, GIVEN BY KING LEWANIKA
Sketch by Von Mugden. Author's collection

more especially the enumeration of the tribes dwelling in the north of his kingdom; these names and other details I wrote at the dictation of M. Jalla. The king had taken the trouble to mark with chalk, or have marked, a rough sketch-map of a portion of his lands on the floor of the hall.

When Lewanika speaks to any one present, the latter must clap his hands. If he sneezes everybody, except of course ourselves, claps his hands. From my seat I could see the dishes of the royal dinner passing through the court, and the natives clapping their hands in their wake;

it is the same with everything that belongs to the king.
As a final question, I asked Lewanika what was the
number of his subjects. He replied that it would be
impossible to give me even an approximate figure.

The sun was on the point of setting when we left the
kashandi. Crossing the public place we saw some great
elongated drums which were about to be beaten in honour
of the new moon. The dancing-men, clad in leopard
skins, were already beginning their terpsichorean exercises
—veritable dislocations.

We are at the beginning of the *mbumbi*, or hot season.
November is the hottest month of the year; at this time
the thermometer has, it appears, registered as much as
118° F. in the shade. The nights are cool, and the
difference between the day and night temperatures is
on an average 36° F.

Once again I was present at the evening service for the
catechists at the chapel, presided over by M. Jalla.
Among those present was the young ex-queen Nolianga,
who has left the harem of her own will in order to
embrace the Christian faith, thus losing the greater part
of her material advantages. The native catechists have
divided Lealuyi into two sections, in which they regularly
go about evangelising, penetrating into the households
of the most hostile inhabitants, in spite of the most
unpleasant treatment.

What can I say of this admirable school? What a life
of devotion these missionaries lead, every instant of it
occupied! They still find means to tend the sick. The
advent of a medical missionary would be hailed with joy.*
What obstacles to overcome from a material point of
view! As at the other stations on the Zambezi, the
rectangular house which M. and Mme Jalla live in, its

---

* This want is happily about to be supplied by the arrival of
Dr. de Prosch.

outbuildings, and the church, were built by their own hands.* On account of the havoc caused by termites, the thatched roofs have to be repaired frequently; the same with the walls. All has to be foreseen and calculated beforehand; the cases sent from Europe take a year or longer to reach their destination.

But with all this how cheerful, kind, and hospitable our missionaries are!

Another visit to Lewanika; he knew of my desire to assist at a sitting of the *lekhothla*, in which he himself gives judgment. Although it was already late in the day, he had the signal given on the drums. Lewanika entered the public place, preceded by two natives, one carrying a stool and the other playing the *serimba*, and seated himself at the foot of a rubber tree, while we placed ourselves near him. His musicians (whose instruments include drums or *kangombia* and *serimba* made of hollow calabashes with small tablets of sonorous wood fixed on them, which are struck with a little hammer) place themselves facing their august master at a respectful distance.

The *likomboa*, or personal servants of the king, and the members of the royal family ranged themselves on one hand, the prime minister and other dignitaries on the other.

From all sides came chiefs and subjects, grouping themselves according to their hierarchic order. Women have not the right to appear in the public place during the *lekhothla*.

Very soon over 200 men were squatting on the sand. All, on arriving, knelt down, bowed very low, and clapped their hands. This homage is called *kandulela*.

On their return from a journey the natives come to make the *shoutela* before the king at a distance of 100

* A devoted artisan-missionary, Mr. Waddell, was of great help to them.

ONE OF LEWANIKA'S COUNCILLORS
From a photograph by the Author

paces; this is a very complicated salutation, mingled with cries, and wherein the forehead often touches the dust. Here came one from a distance to ask the king's permission to keep a wild beast's skin which was given him while travelling; without this consent the present would by right revert to the sovereign.

The last rays of the setting sun lit up a characteristic sight. At the *lekhothla* all important questions are submitted to the king, and his judgments are made law. He represents in his sole self the tribunal, the court of appeal, and the court of cassation. It is needless to say that ink and all kinds of procedure are unknown in these regions! As to whether this method ever produces any miscarriage of justice, that is another question.

But what progress has been accomplished already! It would take pages to speak of the beneficent influence of Christianity here, which little by little penetrates and modifies everything. M. Coillard, the courageous champion of the Gospel, opened the country a dozen years ago, and founded in 1892 this station at the gates of Lealuyi, the stronghold of paganism in this part of Africa. He is admirably seconded by his colleagues.

Infanticide, which was formerly practised openly in the capital, is now suppressed. Of two twins one used to be put to death. It was the same with children of sickly constitution.

M. Coillard has also succeeded in suppressing the terrible ordeal by boiling water. The unhappy creature accused of having cast an evil spell over one of his fellows was made to plunge his hands into boiling water; he was then placed forcibly on a rack and given a violent poison; finally, after horrible sufferings, he was burned alive amidst the curses of the crowd about him. It would take a long time to relate the whole of this chapter of horrors.

King Lewanika used to be very superstitious. On the site of the temple where he used to give himself up to his superstitious practices there is now a workshop. The king works there with his own hands. M. Coillard, on his arrival, saw cords formed of creepers stretching from the royal residence to the outskirts of Lealuyi, in order to arrest the evil spirits.

The darkness is dense, and the difficulties numerous, but these hardy pioneers of the Gospel can count many victories already.

M. Coillard exerts a great influence over Lewanika. A Portuguese half-caste slave-dealer whom I saw the other day came here with the intention of demanding the king's permission to cross his country in order to obtain his lamentable merchandise further to the east. The king would not allow him to continue his journey, and forced him to beat a retreat; in thus acting against his own interests, for the slave-dealer would evidently have offered him valuable presents. Is not this, amongst many other examples, a remarkable proof of the marvellous results in this savage king of M. Coillard's counsels?

When my stay is finished I shall descend the Zambezi by canoe as far as Kazungula, a voyage of which I hear marvellous things; I shall also visit the missionary stations of Nalolo and Sesheke.

September 3rd. —King Lewanika has placed a light hunting canoe at my service manned by vigorous paddlers, who make the vessel fly through the water. In this manner I shall be able to travel from Lealuyi to Nalolo in one day, in response to the kind invitation given me by M. and Mme Béguin to visit their station.

Nalolo, a sub-station of the Zambezi mission, was founded in 1894 by M. and Mme Béguin, of Neuchâtel. Mme Béguin is the daughter of M. Charles Porret, professor and pastor, of Lausanne. I am amazed when I reflect that only a year has gone by since M. Béguin pitched his tent on the bank of the great river. To-day he lives in a house built by his own hands, and he will shortly inaugurate his church, of which the construction advances rapidly.*

A superb Federal flag adorns the chief wall of the room which serves as dining-room, and patriotic songs are often heard under this roof. So many miles from one's native land, one is agreeably surprised by these well-known and well-loved melodies!

Nalolo is one of the most important centres of the Borotsi country, being the residence of the Mokwai, elder sister of King Lewanika. A strange anomaly: in this country, where, as in all non-Christian countries, the woman occupies a dependent position very inferior to that of the man, the elder sister of the king has the same prerogatives as her brother, and the same tributes are paid her.†

As the customs of the country demand, M. Béguin conducted me to the Mokwai this morning. We found her in *lekhothla*, where she presides over the deliberations in the open air and administers justice. Squatting on a mat, she made us sit near her; then, after the salutations, she informed me that she was five years older than her brother Lewanika. The expression of her face, as of her brother's, is very mobile. She was clad in cotton-stuff, and a great carved ivory pin was thrust in her frizzled hair. On her right were her prime minister and other dignitaries; on her left, and at a distance, were men re-

* Just as the station had been finished (the work of three years) it was completely destroyed by fire, the missionaries barely escaping with their lives. Nothing was saved—not even clothes.

† She is known as the Mokwai—or mo-Kwai—the Queen, and is always addressed by *masculine* titles and pronouns. *Trans.*

M. AND MME. BEGUIN'S SCHOOL AT NAIMES

From a photograph by the Author

pairing the net employed in the royal fishery—an enormous affair. In front of the queen were the musicians; when she sneezes they immediately, according to etiquette, play their instruments, and everybody claps his hands.

Then we visited the residence, which is like that of Lewanika; the principal hall is carpeted and hung with rush mats. The queen herself does not disdain to weave mats, and work in pottery on occasion. Here we saw some magnificent skins.

Presently we were given a decoction of maize and milk, a drink slightly acidulated. It was served carefully by one of the queen's servants, who, before presenting us with it, removed the smallest particles of corn he could find with a little stick.

After taking our leave we visited the royal granaries, built with earthen walls raised off the ground by stakes and roofed with thatch.

On returning we went into the school connected with the station, where fifty children, amongst them the little daughter of the Mokwai, were singing hymns at the top of their voices.

The queen sent me a present of maize in the course of the day. On the next day she came to take breakfast with M. and Mme Béguin. She wore a light robe, and for the rest was wrapped in a large piece of bright-coloured stuff, with a red turban on her head. I am told that this queen, who I see kneeling in prayer to-day, only a few years ago killed with her own hand one of her aged dignitaries, who did not satisfy her. She inquired if on my return to my country I shall travel by the fire-chariot and fire-ship (railway and steamer).

After the meal the queen embarked in her canoe, in order to overlook personally the work of her slaves, who are cultivating the fields.

The Mokwai's husband, now away, bears the title of

Mokwai Tunga;* he is the intermediary between the nation and herself.

Nalolo contains about 2,000 inhabitants. Conversely to the other important centres of Borotsi, this little town is situated on the right bank of the Zambezi, at the commencement of a wide plain of arid sand, which stretches westward as far as the Linyanti river.

Nalolo has the advantage of possessing abundant drinking-water, which is far from being the case at Lealuyi. The missionaries have neither fruits nor vegetables; in this Nalolo shares the lot of the other stations.

There are a fair number of cattle in the locality, but here, as in the capital, the cattle have to be sent into the forest during the floods; consequently at these periods there is very little milk to be had.

Many insects; one of the most formidable is the *seruy*, the terrible warrior ant, whose closely-packed ranks never swerve from their path. When they enter a house— which often occurs—one must give way to them on pain of being eaten alive. However, it is the termites that work the greatest havoc in this part of Africa; they attack everything except fatty substances. By means of a juicy secretion they cover the objects of their attack with a layer of moist earth, under the shelter of which they can devour books, clothes, &c., at their ease in a few hours.

What a busy life is a missionary's! Besides his numerous and continued occupations, M. Béguin has attended more than 280 patients between June 1st and August 31st.

The Sunday congregation in the chapel averages 250 to 300, including the Mokwai herself.

I have carried away a grateful remembrance of my stay

I.e., Queen's consort. Sometimes called Son-in-law of the Nation.

at Nalolo and the cordial welcome given me by M. and Mme Béguin.

September 9th.—I returned to Lealuyi several days ago, when a conference took place between the Zambezi missionaries, at which there were present M. and Mme. Jalla, who live here; M. Davit, recently arrived from Europe; M. and Mme Béguin, of Nalolo; M. and Mme Goy, of Sesheke; and M. and Mme Louis Jalla, of Kazungula, who did not scruple to brave the dangers of navigation on the Zambezi in order to compare their experiences and to discuss the interests of the mission.

WOODEN FISH-PLATE, GIVEN BY KING LEWANIKA
Sketch by Van Muyden. Author's collection

Although he was seriously ill, M. Coillard was able, thanks to his energy, to be present at several meetings.

It would be impossible to give an account of all the interesting things I saw and heard; but it seems to me that every one must be struck by the absolute devotion to their work manifested by these missionaries, despite the privations which are their daily lot. The results obtained by this handful of Europeans, animated by the spirit prevailing amongst them, are astonishing. Before their arrival this country might justly be called a land of blood, and King Lewanika himself set the example. Was it not he who shortly after M. Coillard's arrival informed him that when he wished to be rid of a chief he would

AT LEALUI: MWE SALA AND SOME OF HER PEERS
From a photograph by the Author

not henceforth shed his blood, but would have poisoned
beer offered him?

This same Lewanika that we see to-day discussing the
precepts of the missionaries, only ten years ago sentenced
one of his brothers, who opposed him, to death by starva-
tion. Still living, his body wrapped in a white shroud,
he received the honours of royal sepulture, and was then
shut up in a hut at the entrance of the capital, there
lingering for five days before dying of hunger.

We have paid a visit to the camp of the Portuguese
half-caste slave-dealer whom Lewanika forbade to penetrate further into his kingdom. He comes from Benguela,
and has with him natives of Bihé. The coiffure of the
women recalls that seen on the ancient Egyptian monu-
ments.

We have lately seen three natives from the east,
perhaps from Gaza. They belong to the tribe of the
Ngungunyane. They are muscular men, and like to
adorn themselves with leopard-skins. They have come
to Borotsiland to obtain the products of the country.

I think I have already stated that Lewanika and his
sister the Mokwai are representatives of the most complete
absolutism. The land, and all that it contains, including
the inhabitants, belongs to them by principle, and not
one of their subjects is free in his actions. For this
reason, accompanied by M. Jalla, I reminded Lewanika
of the promise he made me to give me three canoes and
their crews to descend the Zambezi as far as Kazungula,
according to my project. The king, according to his
custom, receives us very well; he is in the *kashandi*, and
there introduces to us Bumwai, his nephew, quite a
young man, who will accompany the canoes to their
destination.

Every year the king and his elder sister the Mokwai
receive amongst their many tributes a number of children

of both sexes, as a kind of slave, to become their servitors. They distribute the surplus among their chiefs and others. Only the king and queen have power to liberate them: it is thus that through the mediation of M. and Mme A. Jalla the little Kaiaka, to-day their assistant, became a free man. The children of the Barotsi, the ruling race, cannot become slaves.

Among a tribe recently subjected by Lewanika a young man or woman is still bought for seven or eight hoes.

On returning to the station we saw in the distance a group of natives carrying elephant-tusks; they were bearing them to the king, one of whose principal sources

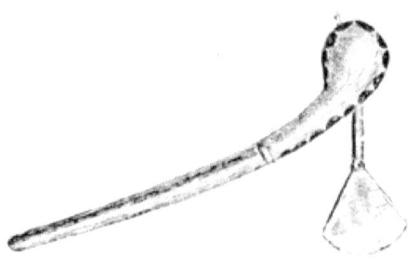

AN AXE, GIVEN BY KING LEWANIKA
Sketch by Van Muyden. Author's collection

of revenue they form. One may reckon that at Lealuyi a pound of ivory is worth five or six shillings.

All wild beasts killed revert by right to the king, with all honey, and the fat of hippopotami. A certain number of canoes are cut in the forest for him, and a certain number of horned cattle, spears, axes, hoes, and grain must be remitted to him every year.

When the tributes are brought to Lealuyi the king at once takes what it suits him to take. The tributes are then carried into the public place, where the king deducts yet another portion. The remainder he then distributes among the chiefs, beginning with the principal ones.

The boatmen, who have received orders to hold themselves in readiness to depart, came to present themselves to-day, so we shall be able to embark to-morrow. These men have to be fed; but, as I have said, the locusts are devastating the country, and there is a consequent famine in the kingdom, so that I should have had very great trouble in procuring the requisite provisions but for the assistance of my hosts, who are so good as to let me have 200 lbs. of maize and millet.

September 11*th*.—Accompanied by M. Jalla I go to take my leave of Lewanika. He is dispensing justice at the *lekhothla*. One of his musicians, an old man, almost blind, sings in a slow, soft voice the noble deeds of his august master.

Lewanika, squatted on a mat, touches our hands; I thank him for all he has done for me during my sojourn in his kingdom. He replies that he will be happy to hear of my safe arrival at Kazungula. He adds that he has sent a messenger to his cattle-stations along the river in order to advise his shepherds that they may be able to furnish me with milk.

I now go to take leave of Katoka, younger sister of the king, and her husband, Mamyumba; the latter is one of the faithful who supported the king at the time of the last revolution, in 1884, when he was obliged to flee from his capital. These revolutions are followed by terrible massacres.

My hosts offer me a basket of sweet potatoes. On returning to the station I receive from the king a *tubana* of curdled milk, and some maize; thanks to these gifts I am for the moment delivered from the fear of famine.

We take a last meal at the venerable M. Coillard's

SERUMBA, AND OTHER ROYAL MUSICAL INSTRUMENTS
From a photograph by the Author

house, at which the king is present in person. I must add that Lewanika has harangued the boatmen, and informed them that that one of whom he received an unfavourable report would be a dead man!

The canoes are loaded, the paddlers are waiting, the moment of departure has come. We prepare to go. How can I thank M. Coillard, M. and Mme Jalla and their friends for their great kindness to me?

A last shaking of hands, a last *au revoir*, and from my canoe I watch Lealuyi quickly disappearing from my sight.

CHAPTER IX

BY CANOE

Descending the Zambezi—The region of the rapids—Sesheke.

THURSDAY, *September 12th.* The flotilla consists of six canoes or dug-outs, three of which are at my disposition. I am in one, Klass Africa and his assistant, Sibuzenga, are installed in another; Watcher, Sibette, and the dog Punch in the third. Provisions and baggage are divided among the three. The three other canoes, which are being sent by Lewanika to Kazungula, are laden with giraffe skins and elephant tusks. The young chief Bumwai, nephew to Lewanika, is in one of these canoes, as he is bidden to accompany the flotilla.

Each canoe is dug out of the trunk of a tree, without a screw or a nail. The construction is the same in all; they vary only in size and navigable qualities.

My canoe, light and rapid, is nineteen feet long by two feet wide, the stern being slightly higher than the prow; the crew consists of four paddlers. The paddle is nearly ten feet in length. It serves at once to paddle and to balance with; the crew stand up and are regular equilibrists, managing to keep the canoe afloat while making it advance rapidly.

Siabusyu, the pilot of my canoe, stations himself at the stern and steers with his paddle. His costume, besides his loin-cloth, consists of a leather collar and a conical straw hat. The second in dignity is called Simakiko, and is in the bow; he it is who keeps an eye always ahead, has to avoid rocks and shoals, and see that we are not surprised by hippopotami; he has three spears ready beside him.

His pretensions in the matter of toilet differ from those of Siabusyu; his loin-cloth, with broad stripes of blue and white, is girt round his waist by a serpent skin, from which hangs also the native pocket-handkerchief, of which I have already spoken. He wears a necklace of transparent beads, two bracelets, of which one is in elephant hide, and feathers stuck in his hat.

The other paddlers, Mukudu and Wichimbamtcha, stand a little astern of the waist of the canoe. They have to regulate their strokes by those of the man standing at the bow.

I have just room aft of Simakiko to sit down, or rather to stretch myself out, on some rush mats. I have another mat overhead to preserve me more or less from the rays of a tropical sun; my baggage serve as cushions. Beside me are my guns; hippopotami are very numerous in these parts, and often attack canoes.

Above all, the most important thing for the *voyageur* is not to move. A mere nothing will capsize a Zambezian canoe.

We are following the Liaboa canal;* the water is low and the boatmen have often to jump overboard to get off sandbanks. The rest of the flotilla remains behind; I have my blankets spread for the night under a large tree, and we light a fire.

September 13th. We are still navigating the canal;

---

* This canal was opened by command of King Lewanika when M. Coillard, after unimaginable difficulties, had cut a first canal connecting Sefula with the Zambezi.

a great number of aquatic birds of all sizes, and with bills
of the most various shapes, inhabit the banks. I admire
a colony of enchanting birds with glittering plumage
wherein purple and blue predominate; a number of holes
dug at regular intervals in the banks serve them for nests.

To catch fish, the neighbouring natives make dams of
reeds across the current. We come across other fishermen in canoes even frailer than ours, armed with long,
flexible spears, with which they transfix the inhabitants
of the water with astonishing skill.

In the course of the forenoon we reach the Zambezi
itself. At the point whereat we enter it the magnificent
volume of its waters flows slowly and with majesty.
We see two hippopotami a little way off. After several
hours we come to Nalolo, far in advance of the other
canoes, which come up much later.

Mokwai sends me milk, fresh and curdled, and I go to
thank her. On my return she sends as escort one of her
servants, who presents me with an ox, her second
present. Rather an embarrassing gift, but a windfall for
my men, who are not long about killing it. I go to seek
a well-deserved rest in one of the rooms of the missionary
station which M. Béguin, at present at Lealuyi, is good
enough to place at my service. And I am just going to
sleep when an invasion of ants makes me clear out as
quickly as possible!

September 14th.—This morning we resume our voyage.
The width of the river varies between three and four
hundred yards. The banks are bare; several villages of
round thatched huts merge themselves in the tint of the
landscape; not a tree to be seen. Abundance of cattle;
and, thanks to the orders given by Lewanika to the chief
Bumwai, I have milk in plenty. We have seen twenty
hippopotami; as a rule they only thrust their monstrous

heads above water for a few minutes, in order to breathe noisily, and then plunge, only to reappear. The boatmen are greatly afraid of them; they make numerous detours to avoid them, or, if that is impossible, they forge very quickly ahead. I have also seen several crocodiles and many aquatic birds, in particular a superb flight of ducks.

The afternoon is already on the wane, when we suddenly sight a canoe containing a white man. He is coming in our direction. It is Captain Gibbons! We shake hands heartily, and very soon, despite the burning sun, the tea-urn is singing on the bank. Pony, who is acting as cook, has stuck his red cap on the very summit of his head, an unquestionable sign of great heat. Gibbons informs me that he has got behindhand in his journey; he is being paddled as quickly as may be to Lealuyi, where he must tender his homage to the king, after having performed his special work in these regions; he will then seek to return with all haste in order not to miss the general *rendezvous* fixed at Kazungula. Will he arrive in time?—that is the question.

I learn, among other incidents, that he has been at close quarters with a lioness, whose skin he is bringing back. But the time flies, and each must resume his route, in the hope of speedy reunion. At nightfall we camp on the sand of the right bank of the Zambezi.

After order has been established in the camp, Klass Africa tells me his canoe passed near a mother hippopotamus with her young one on her back; she offered him a scarcely amiable welcome by opening a formidable gullet, which gave new arms to the paddlers!

September 15*th.*—Sunday, a day of rest. At noon it was 100° F. in my tent. My men rapidly threw up some huts on the beach to gain shelter. At nightfall swarms

I MEET CAPTAIN GIBBONS
From a photograph by the Author

of flies elected to establish themselves in my tent; in spite of all my efforts it was impossible to dislodge them.

Monday, September 16th.—We had only been three hours on the way when, to my astonishment, the canoes pulled up on the right bank and, without orders, the boatmen stepped ashore. I asked the reason for this of the chief Bumwai, who replied that we were near Matongo, in which locality is the tomb of Moana-Mbinyi, the celebrated Borotsi chief, and his men must halt here to pay homage and obtain a fortunate voyage. They did not go as far as the tomb, which was at some distance; Bumwai placed himself at their head, and they gathered in front of a little reed hut built on the bank of the river, occupied by the guardian of Moana-Mbinyi's tomb. They crouched before him, and then, beginning their devotions, clapped their hands and cried aloud, all the while bowing profoundly.

Further on the boatmen wished to halt afresh, this time simply to take snuff. As I knew by experience that one must be firm, especially in the beginning, under penalty of suffering many vexations, they nimbly re-entered their respective canoes.

Three hippopotami; the splendid river flows between banks four or five hundred yards apart. The landscape changes; clumps of trees appear to the right and left; we round the big island of Matanda, which is inhabited, and at midday we halt near the village of Senanga, situate on the left bank of the river, amid a cluster of cocoa-trees. In this place the Zambezi gives the illusion of a lake with numerous tree-clad islets.

In the course of the afternoon we stop on the right bank, at the village of Likomuya. This is the last cattle-station of King Lewanika, and here for the last time Bumwai has some excellent curdled milk brought me.

DESCENDING THE ZAMBEZI. *Drawn by Van Hayden*

More cattle! The tsetse fly comes into its own again; so we shall very soon meet with buffalo, since, as I have mentioned before, the tsetse is met with in the districts frequented by these animals. I need not repeat that wild animals, as well as men, are immune against the sting of the tsetse, which is deadly only to domestic creatures.

On two occasions we met with three hippopotami, sucking in the water and rejecting it noisily, snorting like enormous horses, plunging down and appearing once more at the surface.

The left bank of the river is clad in a dense border of great rushes with white tufts. Before nightfall we shoot the little rapids of Muchia. A hippopotamus salutes us with sonorous but inharmonious grunts. We pitch our camp on an islet covered with white sand, which squeaks underfoot in a curious manner. On a shoal facing us, about two hundred yards away, a pair of hippos are disposing themselves for a night's rest. One of them has his enormous and unaesthetic body almost entirely out of the water. I have heard it said by a very experienced African hunter, that these beasts will often charge on terra firma; but a mere nothing will stop them, as their structure does not permit them to step over the least obstacle.

As far as Senanga we were in the Borotsi plain. The river banks are more or less denuded; the country is a wide plain, with numerous villages and cattle-stations. On leaving Senanga we are in the Borotsi gorges. The ranges of hills on either bank draw close together; the river, cut up by numbers of islets, more or less wooded, divides into several branches. The landscape is picturesque; there are a few little rapids.

September 17th.—We were soon paddling along a

veritable canal, framed in foliage that drooped gracefully
into the water, and passed by the left of the large wooded
island of Mbeta. On account of the exigencies of the
navigation, which is very difficult, we shall often be
obliged to cross from one bank to the other. At nine
o'clock we were on the left bank, at the embouchure of
of the Lui river, which I have already noticed. Here we
lost an hour through a boatman who declared he was ill,
and wanted to be tended in a neighbouring village. In
all probability his indisposition arose from the fact that
we were rapidly approaching the region of the dangerous
Seoma rapids. We threaded our way past a group of
tree-clad islands, through which the great river twists
and winds.

At midday we reached the embouchure of the river
Katangi or Limanika, which derives its source, if I am
not mistaken, from the Kamba lake, which I passed on
my way to Lealuyi. We glided beneath a bower of
foliage; my canoe touched a shoal and heeled over considerably.

At the moment of halting the men take out a long pipe
with a wooden stem, one end of which terminates in a
bowl stuffed with hemp, and the other in a horn which is
filled with water in order to cool the smoke.

One of the boatmen applies his lips to this; inhales
vigorously three or four times, and passes it on to his
neighbour; a pinch of snuff immediately completes the
first operation, and then come sneezes and violent coughs
that seem as they would never finish.

In the afternoon we shot the Mulungu rapid, below
which the river spreads and forms a lake of gracious outlines. The banks are tree-clad and undulating; here and
there are islands covered with bushy foliage. At sunset
two hippopotami came to trouble the silence of drowsy
nature.

September 18th.—We reached Sioma, on the right bank, early in the morning. We were at the entrance to the region of the rapids properly so called. To avoid the impassable falls of Gonye the canoes were unladen, drawn ashore, and dragged over a stretch of nearly three miles by their crews; they were then again floated and loaded up. King Lewanika has established two chiefs at this place to superintend the portage of canoes—Sekomi and Mokwala.

I know by experience that the axiom "Time is money" is not put into practice on African soil. I asked Bumwai to send for the two chiefs, and then, as they did not appear, to go himself. Two hours elapsed; at last they turned up with several of their subjects.

Sekomi is bald, a very rare thing in a native. To-day, after the proper salutations, which are greatly varied in this country, several of the boatmen went up to kiss the chief's right hands. Sekomi informed me that I must remain four or five days at Sioma, "for," he said, "there is a great famine, and my men are scattered through the country in search of food."

This did not enter into my plans at all, and Sekomi's crafty face convinced me that I must use him with authority. His arguments were reduced to nothing. "What are you here for?" I said; "you are no chief if you can't make your men march." He finished by promising that the canoes should be drawn up on the bank to-morrow. "I have your word." "It is well," he replied.

The camp was pitched under a fine *mochaba*, a kind of fig-tree, with a light bark and very soft wood. This tree was nearly forty feet in circumference, and was enlaced with a creeper with white flowers, whose form and perfume recalled jasmine; some dwarf palms grew at its base. When once everything was in order, and my mind in repose, I examined the delightful landscape at leisure.

THE PORTAGE.
From a photograph by the Author.

In front of us the Zambezi split up into several arms, in the midst of which were islands. The river turns sharply to the south-east to form the Gonye Falls, which we approached. We crossed one of the arms of the river by jumping from stone to stone, and so reached the fall itself. From the enormous stones of the left bank, on which we were standing, we watched the river boiling among the rocks ; in the centre it formed a huge foaming, seething whirlpool. By the right bank there is a vertical fall of about eighty feet, and the whole falls must be over 200 yards wide. Splendid as the spectacle is, it is doubtless not to be compared with that awaiting us in a few weeks' time at the Victoria Falls, or the Zambezi Falls properly so called.

On returning I shot a crocodile which was idly stretched in the sun. We learned that just recently a canoe manned by natives, who were ascending the stream, was drawn into the rapids ; two children were lost.

Sekomi warns us that in descending the river we shall encounter mother hippopotami with young ; they are very dangerous. It appears that when the young hippopotamus is born the mother makes a refuge for it among the rushes at the waterside, and if by mishap a canoe approaches it, she will rush upon it to dash it to pieces. After a few days they carry their young on their backs. Besides this, as every one knows, hippopotami can remain several minutes under water, and it often happens that on coming to breathe at the surface they will capsize a canoe

September 19*th*.—Sekomi has kept his word ; on the day appointed his men arrived to drag the canoes ashore. The neighbourhood of Scoma is unhealthy ; fever claims many victims here. At five minutes' distance from the camp we came upon a great level tract, where we found a quantity of graves scattered among the brushwood; they were round, and covered with *débris*. Objects pertaining to the deceased are broken over his grave. Here wooden vessels indicate the resting-place of a man, for only men make these utensils; there the shards of pots show us a woman's grave, for only the women work in clay.

Further on the tail of a buffalo fixed in the earth at the end of a staff told us of the last home of a hunter; to another grave the hut of the dead man had been carried and there burned, a sure sign that in his life he was an evil man, for in so acting his kinsmen believe they can prevent his return to the world. Ale and grain are often spilt over these graves for the use of the dead.

It is a dismal thing to think of; as soon as a man is in a dying state his grave is dug, and sometimes he is put in the earth with the death-rattle still in his throat.

Fever and small-pox are the maladies that most afflict the natives. Sekomi tells me that ten of his children died of small-pox. The only remedy employed is that of dipping the patient in water at the most critical point of the disease. Obviously only robust individuals can resist this energetic treatment. Sekomi, like the greater part of his compatriots, carries on his face the deep scars left by this terrible disease.

September 20th.—I have given the chief three *setsiba* (fathoms or ells of white calico) for the portage of my canoes, and all was ready to start. We embarked in the forenoon. After paddling for some hours we passed the embouchure of the Lumbi river, which makes its junction with the Zambezi in a rather tumultuous manner. A superb goose made an excellent diversion in the daily fare. We were harassed by the tsetse fly. This evening we noticed a great number of buffalo tracks around the camp. We caught sight of three, but the night put a stop to our pursuit.

September 21st. The sun rises above the horizon; Klass and I land on the left bank to track a buffalo wounded the night before. We rejoin the canoes after they have passed through the Kali rapids, and on our return we hear of an adventure that befell Watcher, my Mokololo cook, a boy of an independent spirit, and, I must confess, also very brave. This adventure might very well have been his last. While I was tracking buffalo with Klass, Watcher had himself put ashore on the right bank of the river, without having asked my permission. Quite unarmed, he was walking along the bank, when he suddenly found himself in the presence of two lions, which were gorging on the carcase of a buffalo. He survived the meeting by remaining perfectly still. Let us hope the lesson will be salutary—but I doubt it.

We shoot the Bumbui rapids, the most important that we have hitherto met with on our journey. The Zambezi narrows and roars, breaking through the rocks. The boatmen throw themselves into the water, and in the more difficult passages pass the canoes down one by one, managing them with great skill by means of cords made of palm leaves hitched on the bow and stern. Little by little the Zambezi widens until it is five hundred yards wide, and once more gives us the illusion of an enchanting lake whose tranquil waters are dotted with numerous islets.

As on the preceding days, the tsetse torments us. Although man is immune to the venom of this insect, which is hardly larger than a house-fly, its bite is nevertheless painful.

At sunset buffalo are signalled; Klass and I land on

THE KABA RAPIDS.

Drawn by A. Forre, from a photograph by the Author

the right shore. We get close to a buffalo half-concealed in the scrub. I fire. Quick as lightning the wounded beast makes a semi-circle and charges us at full speed, head down, tail up. Klaas, a few paces behind me, cries out in English, "Look out, they are coming!" Three other buffalo, which we had not seen, and which were grazing in a dip of the ground to our left, attracted by the report, come up at a gallop, pass me at right angles a few paces away, and drag with them the furious brute, which was on the point of reaching me.

Not a sparrow falls to the ground without the will of Him who holds our lives between His hands.

Shortly after we killed the buffalo we were tracking. This beast must weigh between one and two thousand pounds. He is cut up by the light of the moon. This abundance of meat fills the boatmen with joy, although it is far from being appetising, having a very pronounced flavour. The next day is Sunday; on all sides *biltong*—long strips of flesh—is drying in the sun, hung on improvised frames. With the hard work the men have to undergo this food is far from being a mere luxury.

Three hippopotami disport themselves in the river facing the camp.

September 23rd.—We embarked in the canoes early this morning and passed through the blue waters of the beautiful river amongst the green islands and islets. The boatmen love to hold races among themselves, encouraging one another with shouts; but nevertheless they are not above slackening their pace to chatter, laugh, and, above all, to exchange pinches of their disagreeable snuff. This they keep in a little calabash hung at the waist.

I saw the man at the bows, his tapering lance in hand, impale with remarkable dexterity a large fish, called by the natives *dombai*; its yellowish and very succulent

HUNTING BUFFALO
Drawn by Van Ingen

flesh furnished me an excellent meal at the embouchure of the Njoko, where we made our usual midday halt.

We afterwards negotiated several rapids; the most important were those of Lusu, which the natives call the Death Rapids: a European was drowned there some years ago. My men exhibited admirable skill and presence of mind; with straining muscles they avoided the hidden or visible rocks and the treacherous eddies. The least unforeseen shock would capsize our frail vessels. And how they took advantage of the current! They have a holy terror of the hippopotami, which abound in these places.

We saw a cloud of locusts passing. The boatmen, on the alert as ever, found a small green crocodile in the rushes; they dragged it on to a neighbouring islet and there killed it. They will regale themselves on its flesh to-night; they are especially fond of the tail.

We camp above the Ngambwe Falls.

September 24*th.*—The mosquitoes tormented us last night; I am covered with bites. This morning, in order to pass the falls, which are not navigable, the canoes were once more unloaded, drawn up on terra firma, and hauled along, this time for a short portage, and reloaded. This is a very interesting operation; all the boatmen apply themselves to one canoe, and haul it along, accompanying themselves with rhythmic chants.

The landscape at the Ngambwe Falls is noteworthy; enormous rocks form a natural barrier across the river, over which the waters plunge foaming and breaking. The river is very wide, and is dotted with a number of islets covered with vegetation; here and there are palm-trees.

Before noon we had finished, and shot a number of rapids, at which the men rivalled one another in skill;

they use their long paddles as balancing-poles. The most serious rapids were those of Manyekanga.

We camped on a sandy island which makes one of the Katima-Molilo group—literal translation, "fire-extinguisher." At the present moment the men are rapidly erecting the tent; order is promptly established. I admire the ingenuity with which the men in a few

NEAR LUSHU: THE DEATH RAPIDS
From a photograph by the Author

minutes improvise shelters for the night. They cut rushes and interweave them among their paddles, which are thrust into the ground, thus forming a breastwork. The fires are quickly lit, and the earthenware kettles are put on them. What a cheerful race! As usual, pinches of snuff are constantly exchanged, and "Eh! eh! ah wah! ah wah!" resound from all sides.

I notice that when the men have quarrels among themselves they do not last long.

Klass often tells me of episodes in his career of twenty years of African hunting—a career that he began under his father when he was fourteen. He has, it appears, killed two hundred elephants, twenty lions, &c. He confirms what I have already read, that buffalo hunting is considered one of the most dangerous of sports, and assures me that I had a very narrow escape from death the other day.

September 25th. To avoid the great rapids of Katima-Molilo, we entered a channel where the canoes remained for some time grounded on the pebbles. The men had no easy task. We found deep water again, and paddled under the shadow of dense foliage. Presently we encountered eight hippopotami.

The region of the rapids was past, the landscape less picturesque; the banks became bare and low; the great plain stretches on either hand; in a word, the country is like that we passed through above Seoma.

A stiff breeze; the river rough; great sandbanks. We passed near Sekhosi village; cattle grazing in the neighbourhood.

We embarked at the usual time this morning.

Numbers of waterfowl; a goose enriched my larder. At nine o'clock we were stopped by a band of nine hippos, which barred our passage. Klass and I were obliged to land on a sandbank and open fire in order to clear the way; no easy thing, as they were about as much disturbed by our bullets as if they had been pebbles. The boatmen made the canoes fly through the water; fear gave them new strength. We saw three crocodiles.

THE CHICOMBI.
From a photograph by the Author

It would be hard to say how many times already during this voyage I have heard my men pronounce, with varying degrees of vivacity, the words *koubou* (hippopotamus) and *kwaina* (crocodile). Certainly these animals occupy an important place in their thoughts.

At three o'clock we arrived at Sesheke, after winding among the islands formed by the branches of the Zambezi.

Watcher, my cook, tells me that he very well remembers to have seen Livingstone at Sesheke, he being then a child.

September 26th. M. Goy, the missionary, and Mme Goy, of Vevey, whose acquaintance I lately had the pleasure of making at Leahuyi, whither they had gone for the meeting I spoke of, have very kindly arranged for me to stay at their station, although they themselves will not return for some days. I was very well received by the Mosuto evangelist, Aaron. Poor Klass Africa receives bad news here; his wife and his brother-in-law have both died in his absence. In this country, more than in others perhaps, the life of the most robust seems to be a fragile thing.

Sesheke has always been an important centre. Fifteen chiefs have their residence there. The Princess of Sesheke is Akamangisa, daughter to the Mokwai of Nalolo, and niece to King Lewanika. According to custom, I went to present myself to her and to her husband, Mokwa. The sun had already set when I arrived. They received me in the courtyard of their dwelling, where there was a good fire burning. They are both quite young. A broad black line is neatly drawn down the centre of the princess's forehead and round both her eyes; she is clad in a red and green fabric. She whispers to her husband what he has to reply to me. I offer a

blanket as a present; after a few minutes an otter-skin is given me in return.

September 27th.—This morning I received a large vessel of curdled milk; Akanangisa and her husband Mokwa came to return my visit. The weather was rather cool, and they were both wrapped in splendid fur mantles.

Sesheke is on the bank of the Zambezi, at this point fairly high. The crocodiles are an absolute plague here. Some years ago, when Sepopa was king, malefactors used to be thrown into the river; the crocodiles have retained their taste for human flesh. They commit misdeeds without number, and are always on the watch at the watering-place. They wait for the moment when their victim stoops to give the unlucky creature a violent blow with the tail, whereupon they turn quickly, and drag their prey under water to drown. Two native children from the station disappeared in this manner; one while it was washing, while the second, who was playing with some other children, was carried off under the eyes of its companions. A young girl going to fill her pitcher suffered the same fate. The natives believe that crocodiles are departed human beings, who return under this form to torment the living; they will even point them out as So-and-so, of such a village!

Sesheke is in the territory of the subject Masubia tribe, which extends from Seklasi to above Kazungula, comprising the country lying in the triangle formed by the Zambezi and the river which many maps wrongly call the Chobe. It is really called Kwando in its upper course, and Lanyanti from the ancient capital of the Makololo to its affluence with the Zambezi near Kazungula.

M. Coillard arrived first at Sesheke in 1878; he met here the Portuguese traveller, Serpa-Pinto, then sick of a fever; he conducted him to Leshoma, where he tended him, and thence to Mangwato (Bechuanaland). Major Serpa Pinto dedicated one of his volumes concerning this exploration to M. and Mme Coillard in remembrance of all their kindness on his behalf.

M. Coillard and M. Jeanmairet founded the missionary station at Sesheke in 1885; M. Goy, who arrived in Africa in 1885, undertook the superintendence of the station some time after. Much might be said of the devoted and courageous missionary of Sesheke, who saved the life of the English missionary, Mr. Baldwin, whom the natives accused of sorcery and were going to use with violence. This flourishing station has an average of twenty-four catechumens and fifty school children; on Sundays the pretty chapel is filled with an audience of about 150 people, not excepting the Princess Akanangisa and her husband Mokwa.*

September 28th.—In the morning we took to the canoes again. Rato, an influential chief of Sesheke, came to see us off. The unpleasing head of a crocodile emerged from the water; shortly after we saw two others basking in the sun. Three hippopotami saluted us with their snorts. At eleven o'clock, hurrah! we reached the affluence of the Machili, whose course we followed up to the source.

From the bank I could see at a distance of two or three miles the clump of trees near which the Kasaia flows into the Machili before the latter joins the Zambezi. We established one of our first camps near there when first we entered this country. Klass Africa tells me that the Machili is the only tributary of the Zambezi between Lealuyi and Kazungula inhabited by hippopotami.

Further on the river is divided into two arms by the island of Kativa.

* M. Goy died at his post on March 25, 1895, at the age of thirty-three, of the fever of the country.—*Author.*

How many birds there are on the banks of the Zambezi! One of the most common is the fish-eagle, perfectly white except for the black wings. The Zambezian boatmen know how to employ this fine bird to furnish their own larders, as I have seen with my own eyes. When the eagle has seized a fish and retired to the bank to devour it, they throw a stick at its feet with great dexterity. The frightened bird takes flight, usually abandoning its prey.

What a variety of waders!—from the pelican with its abnormal bill down to tiny little birds that can scarcely be distinguished against the soil. A flight of ducks passes over us; let us hope they will prove as succulent as they are beautiful. The head is half white, half black, the throat reddish-brown, the wings and breast black, and the sides ash-coloured. Before erecting the tent for the night we pass the embouchure of the Ungwezi river. There are plenty of crocodiles in the neighbourhood. While encamping we sight three, which disappear under water upon our firing at them.

September 29th.—Early this morning a native came to me with a kind of flat-fish for sale; the name I do not know, but it is far from being as good as the delicately-flavoured *dombai* we had the other day.

We glided through a maze of islets belonging to the Mambova group; they, as well as the banks, were largely overgrown by tall, graceful reeds with white plumes. The hills drew closer together again, and we came to the Mambova rapids, the last before we reach Kazungula. We entered them; suddenly my canoe, which was leading, touched the side of a big rock. In a few seconds we heeled over, and the water ran over the gunwales. We had to rescue my personal effects and devote the day to a general search on the neighbouring bank, which was soon adorned with the most various objects. Our task was facilitated by the heat of the sun; at four in the afternoon all was in order again. There was no serious damage, except to a certain number of photographic negatives which I had brought so far only with great trouble and which have had a most unfortunate bath. I established myself in a native hut, and there, despite the heat of the day, I opened the boxes one by one and changed all the papers which seemed to be damp; I hope to have saved a good number by this means. Finally, after a meal, we set out again. Bumwai seems annoyed at this adventure. This youthful chief, with a mobile face which is always smiling, is interesting; he has a great desire to do right. A tuft of the white hairs of some wild beast is fastened in his frizzled hair. He changes his toilet several times a day; the first thing in the morning he proudly wears an ample fur mantle; later on he throws a piece of red and white cotton over his shoulders; his favourite costume being a shirt and a waistcoat. Like the general run of his compatriots, he prefers to have his head uncovered; but he certainly feels that it adds to his dignity to wear, from time to time, a soft coffee-coloured felt hat adorned with a large black ostrich feather.

CHAPTER X

THE GREAT CATARACTS

Return to Kazungula and Visit to the Victoria Falls.

ONCE again the river grew majestic and calm. On September 30th, early in the morning, I sighted the thatch roofs of the Kazungula mission station; here behold me once more at the place by which we entered the kingdom of the Barotsi, and by which we shall leave it.

M. and Mme Louis Jalla are still at Lealuyi; but I have the pleasure of finding at Kazungula M. and Mme Boiteux, of Neuchâtel—missionaries quite recently arrived. We made one another's acquaintance at Palapye when they too were *en route* for the Zambezi. I am delighted at the prospect of the few days I shall spend with them. They instal me comfortably in their big waggon.

I learn that Pirie has had dysentery; he has preceded Reid by a few days, and has made his camp on the right bank. I send a note to him immediately to learn if I can be of any service to him. Not an hour has passed when I hear two familiar voices: Reid has turned up this morning for the *rendezvous* agreed upon, and has crossed the river with Pirie, who is very much better, to shake hands with me; and a cordial handshaking it was! Then, according to the contract I had made with my boatmen, I give each of them a cotton sheet and a *setsiba* of white calico in payment of their services. To the young chief Bumwai I offer my own blue and red blankets; he brings me in return his terra-cotta drinking-cup.

M. and Mme Boiteux give us the pleasure of re-uniting the three of us at the midday meal. We decide—Reid, Pirie, and I—to set out on foot, at the end of the week, on a visit to the famous Victoria Falls. From thence we shall pass by Panda-Matenga, and at Gazuma-Vley we shall find again our horses, oxen, and waggons; we expect shortly afterwards to be rejoined by Captain Gibbons.*

TERRA-COTTA CUP OF THE CHIEF
BUMWAI, LEWANIKA'S NEPHEW

Sketch by Van Muyden
Author's collection

October 2nd.—The arrival of Prince Litia, who has latterly been absent from his residence, was announced by the public crier, and we set out—M. and Mme Boiteux and myself—for the native village, to witness the honour shown the prince on his return. The chiefs were already in the public place awaiting their lord and master with characteristic patience. The principal chiefs were: Indi, with tip-tilted nose, who states he can make

---

* He was unable to rejoin us in time, for he also had no lack of misfortunes. Not only was he prostrated by fever and dysentery, but on his return he was near falling into the hands of the cruel Matabele, who were then in full revolt. In short, we did not meet again until we were both in London, and were able to exchange impressions at the dinner given us by the Geographical Society. *Author.*

the rain come at will; Momballa, the king of the crocodiles, who flatters himself that he has a special power over these beasts, which has not, however, prevented one of them from recently carrying off a cow of his; and Lukuku, a Christian, and the prince's favourite.

The princess, Litia's only wife, at the head of a procession composed of her retinue and relatives and the wives of chiefs to the number of some 150, advanced to take up her position under a tree near the river.

The chiefs and notabilities of the place formed a group of nearly equal size, and remained apart.

The prince's caravan was signalled at a distance. According to the custom of the country, the women went down to the river in order to sprinkle themselves with water, and then returned to the rear of the men, who kept in front when Litia approached. Then, according to Borotsi etiquette, they gave the salutation called *shoaluba*, shouting and holding their hands in the air; they then sat on their hams and bowed, repeating the whole process many times.

The women crouched down and prostrated themselves, without raising their hands in the air, all the while crying out salutations to the welcome one. The two groups joined the prince's following and entered the public place, where the salutations already described began again. After this the women dispersed, while the men remained in *lekhothla* to hear what the prince had to say to them—important matters, it appeared, which must not reach the ears of a stranger.

A few drops of rain began to fall, the first since our arrival in the country. The atmosphere was scorching; rain would be welcome. Alas! it was only momentary!

October 3rd.—I slept only an hour last night, in order to arrange my notes, travelling journal, and daily log.

THE GREAT CATARACTS 189

No one would believe the difficulty of doing this work regularly in the life we lead.

October 4th.—The chief Rato, a confidant of King Lewanika, arrived from Sesheke to-day. His master wanted us to exchange some of our surplus lead and

THE ELEPHANT TUSK OF 75 LBS.
From a photograph by the Author

powder against an elephant tusk of 75 lbs. weight. Out of deference to the missionaries, we were not willing to effect the exchange until we had consulted them on the subject.

I had the privilege of accompanying M. and Mme Boiteux and Mdlle Kiener on one of their evangelizing rounds. In particular, we visited a poor old blind woman, to whom the young girls educated at the station bring part of their food; they are clubbing together to adopt the destitute! A real miracle, to those who know the blacks.

As at Lealuyi, Nalolo, and Sesheke, I did not know how to thank the missionaries of Kazungula for their hospitality, and for all they have done for me. The always sorrowful moment of departure arrived; the mission children came to salute me by these words: "*N'tate lumela*" ("Goodbye, father"); "*Sala hantle*" ("May it be well with you").

My readers will perhaps allow me, as I am leaving Borotsiland, to resume in a few lines my impressions of the work accomplished by the missionaries in these savage countries.

All must recognize that M. Coillard was happily inspired in setting to work upon this important people the Barotsi, whose vassals are all the neighbouring tribes.

It was he who first came in 1884 to found this mission, in the face of unheard-of difficulties, in which he has been so well seconded by his colleagues. To-day the Barotsi Mission,* which, as every one knows, is affiliated to the general work of the Evangelical Mission of Paris, counts six European missionaries and six or seven black Basuto evangelists.

I one day heard M. Coillard say that at the present time fourteen European missionaries and thirty native evangelists are wanted, so as to be able to occupy the important points of the country before the arrival of the white adventurers, who too often dishonour the name of European. But for this purpose the foundation of an

<small>Known in Switzerland and France as the Zambezi Mission, but distinguished as the Barotsi Mission in England, as there are several others on the Lower Zambezi.</small>

evangelical and an industrial school in this country would be necessary. However, eight young Barotsi are already sufficiently well prepared to form a first nucleus of an evangelical body.

In Europe we cannot, with the best will in the world, form an idea as to what the life of a missionary really is in this country. No one but a traveller who has seen what it is with his own eyes can give any faithful account of it.

It is not sufficiently understood that, from a material point of view, the missionary has no one to count on but himself. He must be at the same time his own carpenter, cabinet-maker, blacksmith, architect, and engineer, and he runs short of everything. On the other hand, in addition to his pastoral and educational labours, he must undertake those of a physician and an everybody's counsellor. His door is continually besieged.

How can I recite also the services that the missionaries have rendered to general science, and how as explorers they have increased the field of human knowledge! I must not forget to mention that some years ago the Society of Geography of Paris conferred the honour of a medal upon M. Coillard.

Finally, how can I describe the difficulties and privations which are their daily bread?

Insects of all kinds form a veritable pest: the most formidable are the termites, whose misdeeds I have already told, and the *seruyi*, the warrior ants. Legions of mice and rats cause incalculable havoc; it is the same with locusts and snakes, to say nothing of wild beasts and mosquitos.

Then there is the treacherous sun and the terrible fever, that will strike down the bravest in a few hours.

While I am speaking on this subject I must call attention to the fact that whites who are condemned to a diet of meat and farinaceous foods—we have experienced it ourselves—find their strength declining little by little. I feel that it is my duty to insist that as much as possible of preserved fruits and green vegetables should be sent out to the Zambezian missionaries.

Accustomed as we are from infancy to lack nothing of the necessaries of life, these details may seem perhaps unimportant; only the traveller who has suffered for a time from these privations can understand them.

I must speak once more of the hostility of the chiefs, of the horrors of paganism. Finally, do people ever reflect on the moral isolation of this handful of Europeans, who, thousands of leagues from their native countries, are obliged to see, hear, and resist, in the proportion of one to multitudes, an order of things engendered by the natural evil which exists in the heart of all men who are left to themselves? If we have not suffered this isolation we cannot conceive of it; above all, we who have had the good fortune to be born in a civilised country, and who, all of us, whether we choose to recognise it or not, benefit by the beneficial influence brought upon the earth by Christianity.

In terminating these reflections, I will add that, as an impartial traveller, I found it impossible not to be struck by the complete and absolute devotion of these missionaries to their work, in spite of privations and difficulties that were daily renewed. And with all this, as I have already said, they know very well how to be gay, hospitable, and kindly!

What a living example are these heroic pioneers, never complaining, always at the breach, always ready to pay with their own person! And what a noble task is that of the wives of these missionaries, the worthy rivals of their husbands! What an example is that of a Christian

NEAR THE VICTORIA FALLS
From a photograph by the Author

family to these pagans, amongst whom the woman is so inferior to the man!

How is it that this army of heroes, scattered in the remotest ends of the earth—the missionaries—do not receive more sympathy, and, above all, more material aid? Their work is a civilising work in the most noble and elevated acceptance of the word.

M. Boiteux himself ferried me across the Zambezi in his canoe; on the right bank our last words were "*Au revoir.*"

Towards evening I rejoined Pirie and Reid, who went on ahead yesterday.

October 5th–6th.—We walked from Kazungula to the Victoria Falls, following more or less closely the course of the Zambezi, across a pebbly country, often covered with scrub, undulating, and cut by watercourses on their way to the river. As usual, we had plenty of distractions. One of our men, Watcher, always imprudent, found himself unarmed almost nose to nose with a leopard, which happily was taking its siesta. He told us he had to go down on all-fours in order not to wake the beast, and come out of the encounter safe and sound.

Jonnes, the cook, on one of these days proudly brought us a water-tortoise of eight or ten pounds weight.

During the night especially the mosquitoes waged a desperate war against us, despite the fires lit in front of and around the tent. It was sometimes impossible to sleep, so we sat in the smoke to escape their bites.

October 7th.—In the morning we saw in the distance the mist rising from the Falls, and heard their thunder. To gain an idea of the Victoria Falls * you must imagine the wide Zambezi flowing in its normal manner amid

* The natives call these falls *Musi oa Tunya*, "Thundering smoke." *Author.*

PART OF THE VICTORIA FALLS. *Drawn by G. Vuillier, from a photograph by the Author.*

islets overgrown with palm-trees, and that suddenly it comes upon a fault in the rock, more or less perpendicular, about a mile wide and from 300 to 400 feet in depth. Into this gulf, whose width varies approximately from forty to eighty yards, the whole river leaps, making a turn of almost a right angle with the south-east.

To admire this wonder of nature in all its majesty we placed ourselves on the further side of the gulf, and consequently facing the falls. We marched beneath great trees connected with one another by flexible lianas, inhabited by numbers of monkeys. Here and there were masses of light-coloured ferns.

On turning to the east we came in sight of the first fall, the least considerable in point of volume. Unlike the other falls, its shuddering waters shoot down the rocks in an inclined plane. It is separated from the second fall by Livingstone's Island, so called in memory of the famous traveller who first entered these regions. This second fall is vertical. An island separates this also from the next; but at this part the mist, rising from the thundering of this liquid avalanche, is so great as to make it impossible to distinguish it. This was, in my opinion, the grandest part of the Victoria Falls. It was impossible not to be fascinated by this enormous mass of water, falling tumultuously, rebounding, and shattering itself into dust. It formed an opaque atmosphere before our faces, on which the sunlight played and formed intermingled rainbows of great beauty.

However, as we did not want too much of a bath, we had to tear ourselves away from our contemplation of the falls and continue our walk; for, although the sky is of an intense blue, we were soaked through; at moments rain itself could do no more. The temperature was like that of a hothouse.

Still another island, this time clearly visible, and we

were in sight of the fourth and last fall. It is very wide, and if it does not impress the spectator as much as its sister falls, yet its character is not less striking; its waters are split up by the rocks into a succession of spouts which take the most various forms.

I find it difficult to establish a comparison between Niagara, which I visited some years ago, and the Victoria Falls. Indeed, they are scarcely comparable. Thanks to their great volume of water, the American Falls are perhaps more imposing, whilst the African Falls take the palm from the point of view of the picturesque. But who can imagine the impression produced at the time of the rains by this magnificent spectacle?

We had the pleasure of meeting Dr. Arnold Winkelreid Penther at the Victoria Falls, an Austrian traveller who arrived some weeks ago, and whose stay is not nearly finished. His rear-guard attends him at Tamasetsie in the south. He is justly enthusiastic over this marvellous portion of the Zambezi, and is studying the falls under all their aspects. It was he who was good enough to give me the dimensions cited above, which, he informed me, are approximate.

Dr. Penther has lost twelve of his oxen! This puts him in a critical position.

CHAPTER XI

IN DISTRESS

From the Victoria Falls to Panda-Matenga—The Great "Thirst Trail"—The Gway river (Frontier of Matabeleland) and Bulawayo.

ON the evening of October 8th we struck our tent and took leave of Dr. Penther; the latter, as usual, shared our meal. Another white man arrived unawares, a Mr. R——, since dead.

He told us that he was returning from an expedition into Boshukulumbwe, and that his companion in misfortune, an Englishman like himself, was extremely ill; he had to be carried as well as could be for more than 120 miles.

Moreover, their head boy, a trusty servant, was dying of fever. We gave them what medicines, &c., they had need of. Then we marched until midnight to Panda-Matenga in a southerly direction.

At Gazuma-Vley, near Panda-Matenga, we shall take possession of our ox-waggons once more, as well as the reserve horses left behind, before crossing over to the right bank of the Zambezi.

October 9th.—We marched during part of last night; after a few hours' rest, only too short, as might be expected, we resumed our march at five this morning.

Reid, Pirie, and I, as usual, soon found ourselves a good way ahead of the column. In the course of the day our men lost their way; we had to pass the night as best we could, covering ourselves as well as might be with dry grasses, and keeping close to the fire. The heat continues very great in the daytime, and the nights are very fresh.

October 10th.—We rejoined our column, which went ahead rapidly with Reid and Pirie in search of water. The column was in movement, when for the first time I suddenly felt myself fail. For the first time also I lagged behind, and was obliged to disburden myself of my rifle. I handed it over to the last man of the column, one of the Masaroa. Despite my requests, he would not wait for me, and replied only by these words, which for him summed up the whole situation, *Metsie, metsie!* "Water, water!"

My comrades at the head of the column had no idea of what had happened to me, and I very soon found myself alone in the company of the two dogs, Bless and Punch, who had not deserted me.

The heat was terrible, a perfect furnace, and the scrub on either side of the trail offered no shelter.

I tried to go on, but was repeatedly forced to let myself fall on the burning sand. I was evidently suffering from sunstroke or fever. My respiration became hurried, my tongue swollen, and my sight troubled. As I went forward I seemed to see Reid or Pirie in front of me . . . they disappeared as I approached. Deceitful mirage!

Another mirage: I thought I saw our tent pitched at a short distance. Another cruel deception! All these distressing symptoms grew worse; I was alone, and felt that I was lost. I implored God to help me, and I still had strength to drag myself painfully onwards for an hour. Then my legs failed under me; I could do no more. But my prayer was indeed answered. Just at this moment I saw a few yards ahead a tall baobab tree, the only one met with during the day, and lying in the shadow of its trunk was the man in charge of the bag containing my personal belongings! Tired out, he was resting there, reckoning upon joining the column later. What a deliverance! I stretched myself out behind the trunk, and covered myself up with the clothes contained in my bag in order to protect myself as much as possible from the treacherous rays of the sun.

While waiting for the now assured help, I moved round the tree with the shadow as the sun progressed. At last, at five o'clock, Reid and Pirie arrived; supported by them, I managed to reach the camp, which was pitched near a pool a mile or so further on. Once installed in the tent, Reid applied hot water to my feet and cold douches to the head and spine; this treatment relieved me. It was high time.

Friday, October 11th. Thanks to Reid's energetic treatment, I passed a fairly good night, and this morning I felt able to get into the saddle.

Reid in the meantime had sent to Gazuma-Vley for the horses, where, as I have stated, we left our rear-guard before crossing the Zambezi.

We reached Panda-Matenga at an early hour. Here the British Chartered Company has its most advanced post in this part of the country; it consists of a few mud huts, of which the principal is inhabited by B——, the "field cornet." The latter, seeing my doleful state, offered me hospitality. The hut was divided into two parts; I was put to bed in the part serving as the warehouse for the merchandise, which consisted chiefly of wild beast skins. For bed there was a rough framework set against the wall some two or three feet high, with cross-pieces of sticks covered with straw. During the day there was a constant coming and going of blacks, but I was too ill and weak to pay any attention to them.

In spite of the anguish I suffered the day before, I rashly got into the saddle on the morning of the next day. I was not long in suffering for my foolishness, for an acute crisis set in from October 11th to October 15th. I was for several days in a very critical situation. However, I never lost consciousness, so I was able one day to hear B—— say to Reid, amongst other things, "I thought he was a dead man."

All my blood flew to my head, causing distressful buzzings. I suffered also from excessive sweats, which reduced me to a skeleton; my tongue turned black on several occasions.

I must add that B—— and Reid, recognising the gravity of my illness, did their very best for me with such means as they had at their disposition.

One night B——, who was awake in the room next to mine, and separated from it by a large doorway, suddenly rushed up to me armed with his rifle. "Take this lantern!" he said sharply. I took it with difficulty. A shot rang out at my ear, but in my state of prostration I was indifferent to what was going on around me; Reid had just killed at close quarters a venomous snake which he heard hissing as it entered the hut.

October 15th.—As soon as I was able to stand, the fifth day after being taken ill, the waggons were yoked, and very soon everything was ready for our departure for the south. In this first period of convalescence every effort was a pain to me; the jolting of the waggon and the usual privations of all kinds were not calculated to hasten my recovery. Less than twenty-four hours after setting out we reached Daka pool without accident, and there found water.

Difficulties are about to commence again; the next water we shall find will be that of Tamasetsie. To reach that we have to cross fifty miles of thick sand, troublesome for the oxen—the "Thirst Track," so much dreaded by travellers.

October 18th.—What a day! We were in great distress, amidst the sand, in a torrid heat. The oxen of the large waggon, whose wheels are now almost past work, were unable to go a step further, despite all efforts.

Happily we had behind us Mr. S——, an Irishman, returning from the Victoria Falls; we saw a good deal of him at Panda-Matenga. His caravan consisted of three large waggons and fifty oxen. The latter are smaller and less hardy than ours, and will also have difficulty in crossing the "Thirst Track."

He arrived in the evening. We proposed the following arrangement, to which he agreed: We shall abandon the large waggon in the sands, like a wreck at sea; we offer him a reinforcement of part of our oxen, and he will take charge of those cases for which we have no room in our small waggon, and will be carried in one of his. Here, alas! I have to leave the skin of the buffalo which failed to disembowel me. I had prepared it with care and brought it so far at a great trouble; it weighed seventy-four pounds, and it would have pleased me to be able to offer it to the museum at Geneva.

No sooner said than done, and the oxen thus distributed made a long night march.

October 19th.—As late as between four and five o'clock in the afternoon the thermometer marked over 95° F. in the shade of the waggon. There is no other shade what-

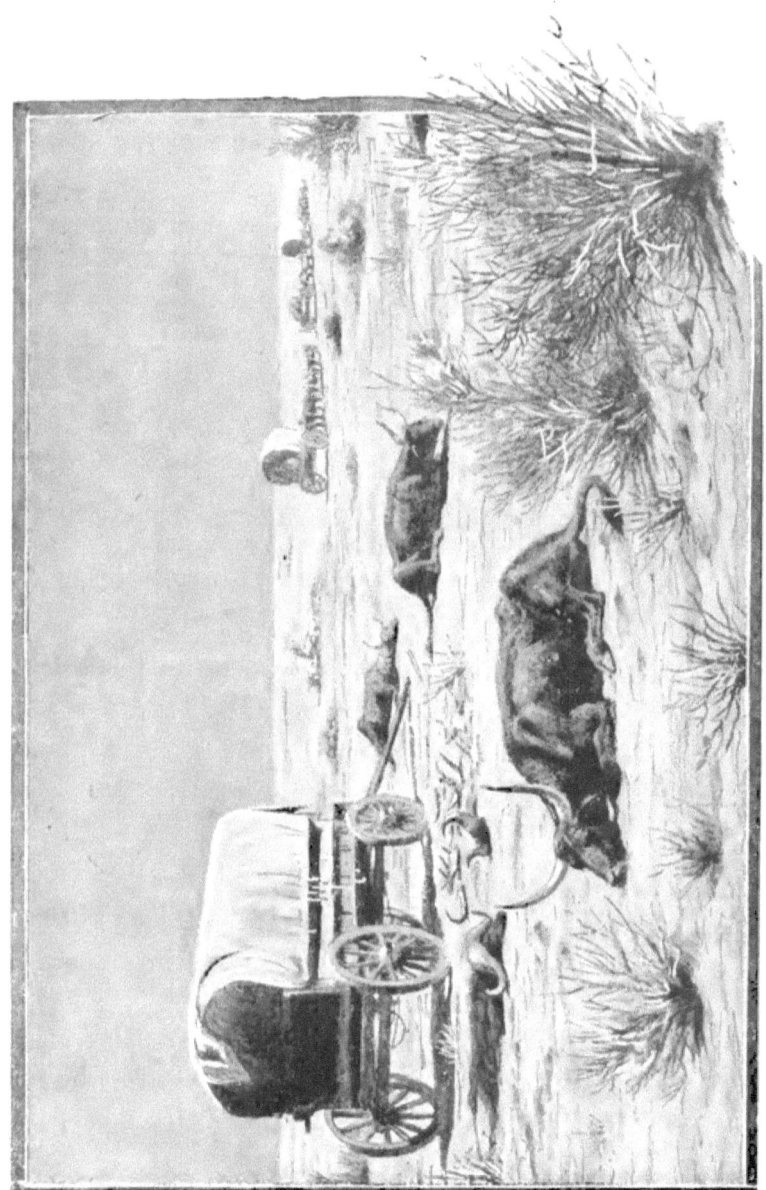

IN DISTRESS! WE ABANDON THE LARGE WAGGON. *Drawn by Van Muyden*

ever; when we halt, we have to seek shelter under the waggons. At night the oxen were in distress, worn out with exertion, and above all, with thirst. At the risk of losing them and of finding ourselves in a desperate position, we were obliged to leave three of the waggons on the spot, with the intention of sending for them later, and to set out as quickly as possible, man and beast, for the Tamasetsie watering-place. After some hours we had to do the same with our sole remaining team, consisting of thirty of the strongest oxen.

October 20th. At sunrise Pirie and Reid set out on horseback for Tamasetsie pool, which, we hoped our men had reached. S—— and I stayed behind with waggon until the evening.

We had an afflicting sight before our eyes; the sad pass of S——'s oxen, the weakest of which were left behind, many did not reach Tamasetsie. Their parched nostrils would never again know the healing touch of water. They shambled round us, and seemed to implore us with their great moist eyes; but we, alas! could do nothing for them. Before sunset, although suffering greatly, I got into the saddle with S——, and late at night we found ourselves all re-united at Tamasetsie with water in abundance. It was time we arrived, for the surviving oxen had been three days and nights without water.

October 21st.—Last night a lion signified his presence in the neighbourhood with magnificent roars. On waking this morning S—— discovered that this unwelcome neighbour had been feasting off one of his finest oxen. He had already lost ten in crossing the "Thirst Track." One of his best oxen went mad when, after long deprivation, it found itself once more in the presence of water;

it died in a few hours without being able to drink. Our expedition was fortunate enough not to leave a single ox behind in the "Thirst Track."

At the Tamasetsie water we found Herr H⸺, a German, in charge of the rearguard of Dr. Penther, the Austrian traveller we met at the Victoria Falls.

As my state was still very serious he made room for me in his camp while Reid, Pirie, and S⸺ went back for the waggons. I shall never forget this man; for a whole week he tended me like a brother. Extremely weak, I spent every day stretched on the ground, wrapped in blankets, and with my head bound with a thick towel always soaked with water; an indispensable precaution in such a case—that is, when the precious liquid can be used without stint.

H⸺ did all that was in his power to shelter me from the rays of the burning sun, and himself prepared my food with what poor resources were at his service.

Our men built kraals in which the beasts were shut up every night. Two giraffes killed in the neighbourhood furnished us with fresh meat; at the end of a week all our belongings were got together again, excepting the first waggon, which was abandoned too far back to allow of going in search of it, having regard to the exhaustion of our oxen.

October 26th.—Reid and I have decided to set out to-morrow night for Bulawayo, the principal town of Matabeleland.

October 27th.—After taking leave of H⸺ we started. We are travelling in the "Scotch cart," a little two-wheeled waggon drawn by ten oxen. Five men accompany us, besides two saddle-horses. We have dismissed the rest of our caravan, who have to get back to

Bechuanaland. Pirie and S— will follow our trail later when the latter's oxen are in good condition; we leave for his own use our surplus oxen, and he will carry part of our baggage for us.

I do not wish to enter into a detailed account of our doings, nor to describe the route pursued in a south-easterly direction from Tamasetsie to Bulawayo; it would take too long.

We have done the distance, with the loss of one animal, in seventeen days—a journey which is commonly reckoned as one of three or four weeks. We had to make a number of marches, by day and by night, across alternations of sand and pebble.

At intervals we met Masaroa who gave us almost perfectly accurate advice as to the trail to be followed, and the places where we should find water. On the whole water was not very scarce on this journey, but it was often muddy. Many flights of locusts; intense heat.

The space available for Reid and myself inside this little waggon is only about five feet six long, four feet six wide, and two foot three high; the temperature taken, at random, is 97°, almost hot enough to boil eggs, and the air is absolutely stifling under the tilt. The shelter given by the scrubs being negligible, we are obliged, during the halts, to construct a " skerm " whether we will or no, if we wish to escape from our narrow prison; but the " skerm " is soon pierced through by the burning rays of the sun.

Although Reid tends me as well as he can, it will readily be understood that a journey under such conditions cannot be made by a convalescent, such as I still am, without all kinds of sufferings. Often I have been obliged to clench my teeth and call up all the strength I was capable of. How much a little rest, a little less violent jolting, fruits, fresh vegetables, or merely pure iced water would have relieved me!

The days go by; at last, on November 11th, we see in the distance the blue line of hills behind which is Bulawayo.

We receive a visit from a number of Makalaka, the former slaves of the cruel Matabele; they are fine-looking men, well set up, and like other tribes do not disdain to adorn themselves with beads.

The physiognomy of the country changes. Goodbye to the plains; we are in the hill-country, and travelling over stony ground, on which our chariot, the body of which rests directly on the axles, bounces inordinately. The going is often difficult, especially across the steep river-beds, such as that of the Gway, whose banks are so steep as to seem to forbid the passage of any kind of vehicle whatever.

On November 10th we step on the soil of Matabeleland. Kraals appear here and there; the trees are thick, and the air is keener; the trail also becomes better. It is time it did so; the weaker of the oxen are reduced to skeletons, and lie down during the marches; then we have to get them on their legs again, and, as the case may be, give them another place in the team. It is distressing to see the poor beasts suffering and hear them moan without its being possible to relieve them; but we must go on, always on! So it is in life. One day Reid had to kill an ox which was positively unable to move further.

November 13*th.*—Towards evening we sight Bulawayo. What a contrast, after our late manner of living, to find ourselves in a few hours' time seated before a relatively well-appointed table, and then to be able to sleep in a real bed! . . .

CHAPTER XII

THE OUTPOSTS OF CIVILISATION

Bulawayo, the chief town of Matabeleland.

THURSDAY, *November 14th.*—When, on his return from uncivilised countries, after all the privations endured, all the risks run, the traveller once more finds himself amid the advantages of civilisation—even in a rudimentary state, as is to-day the case at Bulawayo—accustomed as he is to get out of difficulties of every kind by himself, he is at first quite bewildered by the change. Without speaking of the rest, the dangers continually run, the anxieties as to one's whereabouts, food, and, above all, water, forming the daily preoccupation of this rough African life, which nevertheless has so many charms, for it appeals to the actual nature of man—all this becomes nothing but a dream.

What a change it is, and how easy everything becomes, when one can once more procure the necessaries of life without effort!

How many Europeans who have never quitted their native soil, and who complain of the little imperfections and vexations of civilised life, really understand all the advantages they enjoy!

Here at Bulawayo, as across the sea, every man, even the most miserable, can enjoy without reserve these two blessings which one must have wanted in order to appreciate them at their true value—pure fresh water and good bread.

November 15th.—At Bulawayo our expedition terminates, as was agreed. The remaining horses, oxen, waggons, &c., have been sold in this favourable market. Those of our men whom we engaged up to this time are now disbanded and paid.

AT BULAWAYO
From a photograph by the Author

Kanye, the brave horse on whom I finished our last journey the other day, died suddenly to-day while he was being led by hand—the result of the exhaustion and privations he had undergone.

November 16th.—Everything being finished, Reid, who already knows the south-eastern parts of Africa, goes directly to the Cape *viâ* Mafeking. As for me, I propose to return later by way of the centre of Matabeleland and the Transvaal. After visiting Johannesburg, "the city of gold," I shall embark on the Indian Ocean at Natal.

November 18th-25th.—Since my arrival here I have apparently been presuming too much on my strength, for I have had a bad relapse, and was obliged to enter the Bulawayo infirmary on the 18th. Although I have had to keep my bed all the time, I have appreciated this spell of relative luxury compared with what I suffered before under the same conditions of health. I have been well looked after by Dr. L——.*

November 26th-30th.—Period of convalescence.

December 5th.—Pirie and S—— arrive. It will be remembered that Reid and I left them at Tamasetsie. But—oh, the disappointment!—they announce that they were obliged, on account of the bad state of their teams, to abandon S——'s large waggon at Tamasetsie, the very one containing the collecton I made with so much trouble in Borotsiland, and brought with me with so many difficulties.

S—— tells me he lost ten oxen after our departure, which makes a total loss of twenty-one since leaving Daka, besides several horses. Only three of the oxen we left with Pirie have perished.

Pirie and S——, embarrassed as they were, had altogether much difficulty in reaching Bulawayo. Their journey from Tamasetsie took thirty-two days. "It was hell," Pirie announced.

December 9th.—The loss of my collection is a great annoyance to me. I have learned from experience that

* Since wounded in the Matabele war. *Author.*

in an expedition such as ours the first principle of success is never to be discouraged, come what may, so long as a glimmer of hope remains. So I set to work. Thanks to the kindness of Mr. B——, our agent in Bulawayo, I make an attempt to recover my collections, and finish by finding the necessary man in the person of one Harry, a half-breed. He knows Tamasetsie, and is going to set out to-morrow with a light waggon and six well-conditioned oxen.

I cannot wait for my belongings, but I have given all necessary directions to Mr. B——, so that in case of success the latter can send them to Europe.*

Thursday, December 12th.—I leave Bulawayo to-morrow. This country is still so little known that I cannot set out again without mentioning a few of the observations and reflections which have been suggested by my stay here.

What a proof is the vitality of Bulawayo, a city born yesterday, of the energy of the Anglo-Saxon race! It has not been in existence for two years, and already it makes pretension to consider itself the capital of this new country of Matabeleland. If we go back two years we find that this country belonged to King Lobengula. Thanks to a convention concluded with him the Chartered Company had already for some time occupied the country to the east, Mashonaland, when —it was an unlucky date in the annals of his nation—a party of his people entered Mashonaland unawares and massacred some of the whites

---

* He succeeded. Shortly after landing on European soil I received to my great surprise and satisfaction, the advice of the arrival of a number of my cases at Southampton, so that I was able to exhibit the greater part of my collection at the National Swiss Exposition of Geneva from July 4 to October 14, 1896. What was missing was probably stolen by the natives. *Author.*

living in the little town or camp of Victoria. In 1893 three English columns, composed largely of volunteers, set out from three different points of muster, and inflicted a severe lesson on the Matabele.* Since then their country has been under the jurisdiction of the Chartered Company. Matabeleland is to-day divided into two large districts, Bulawayo and Gwalo, which in turn are split up into several divisions. At the head of each of these great districts is placed an English magistrate, the Civil Commissioner. The central government of Rhodesia—the collective name of Matabeleland and Mashonaland—is at Salisbury, the capital of the latter country.

The traveller who has just left his ox-waggon, at present the only means of reaching this oasis, cannot help thinking that Bulawayo, one of Mr. Rhodes' creations, has high ambitions. Everything has been conceived on a large scale; the streets of this embryonic town intersect one another at right angles, like those of the United States, and have an average width of 100 feet, not counting the side-walks. The land abutting is divided into "stands," or lots 300 feet deep by 150 feet of frontage, which are sold by auction. They are keenly disputed, and sometimes fetch a price that would not be disdained in any European city.

At the present day Bulawayo has the look of an immense camp. At the side of well-built houses of red brick we find cabins of galvanised iron and white tents in picturesque groups. Public conveniences are being organised rapidly; works are already in course of construction to supply the town with drinking-water brought from the neighbouring hills, and to light it by electricity. Besides the administrative buildings, Bulawayo has already four places of worship, a hospital admirably organised, a

* The Matabele are Zulus who emigrated under the head of the great chief Mo-elekatsi years ago. *Author.*

post and telegraph office, a covered market, an exchange, four banks, three schools, a prison, and a central police station; a temperance tavern is also proposed. Then a large space is reserved for athletic sports; here and there we see large stores, veritable bazaars, where the most varied produce and merchandise are found assembled. I must not forget to mention a club; I had the honour of being an honorary member during my stay in the town.

The local press is represented by three papers. Two appear twice a week — the *Matabele Times* and the *Bulawayo Chronicle*. The third, the *Sketch*, an illustrated paper, lithographed, is issued weekly.

Bulawayo will soon possess a municipal council. It is for the moment administrated by the " Sanitary Board," a commission of six members, of whom three are chosen by the Chartered Company and three are elected by the inhabitants.

The right of voting is possessed by every resident holding property or paying twelve pounds a month for board and lodging.

The population — exclusive of the blacks, whose number it would be difficult to estimate, as it varies greatly — comes to about 2,000, mostly Anglo-Saxons. There is perfect order day and night. Putting aside the tenacity and the respect of law inherent in the Anglo-Saxon race, as well as the great liberty accorded to individual effort, one of the principal causes of England's colonising power consists, in my opinion, in the fact that the best elements of the nation do not hesitate to expatriate themselves, the contrary often being the case elsewhere; thus laying the foundation-stones of prosperous colonies, and adding new gems to their crown, already so well adorned.

The picturesque side of this growing town is interesting to watch. Men with bronzed energetic faces go through the streets and about their business in riding

breeches and shirt-sleeves, wearing felt hats with huge
brims. In the saddle they nearly always gallop. Then
there are the prospectors, who, after seeking for gold in
virgin soil with more or less success, arrive from the
interior of the country, tanned by the burning sun and
inured to every privation.

At present waggons drawn by interminable teams of
oxen are the only means of conveyance to Bulawayo.
Nearly all the provisions consumed by the inhabitants are
brought in this manner from Mafeking. According to
the state of the tracks and the height of water in the
rivers to be forded they take from six weeks to four
months in reaching their destination. In consequence it
is no rare thing for such and such an article or provision
to run up to exorbitant prices, and then to be entirely
lacking until the problematical arrival of the next convoy.

The market, attended exclusively by men, is held in the
morning between six and eight. The products of the
soil have to be sold by auction. The culture of fruit and
vegetables is in its infancy. According to the disposition
of the buyers, and the rarity of the product, certain
articles fetch fabulous prices; for instance, two dozen
fresh figs sold for fifteen shillings. Six weeks ago a
cabbage sold for twenty-five shillings, to-day you can buy
these luxurious vegetables for a shilling. Four pounds of
potatoes go for three-and-six or four shillings. At Easter
a dozen eggs were worth sixteen shillings; to-day they
do not exceed half-a-crown or three shillings; a bottle of
milk is rated at two shillings, &c., &c.

It appears that all cultivable land within a radius of
sixty miles from Bulawayo is already sold. The farms—
I have had the pleasure of visiting one—are of an average
extent of three thousand acres.

As for the mines, every resident—or every person
arriving in the country and declaring himself willing to

work—has the right to ten claims measuring 600 feet by 400. The first formality to fulfil is to present oneself at the office of the mines to demand authorisation for prospecting, which is accorded by a stamped licence costing a shilling. The prospector has now the right to scour all Matabeleland; when he thinks he has found a reef of auriferous quartz he returns to the office and has his claim registered. By this he becomes the "owner prospector" of the claim; he must further, within three months, dig a shaft of a certain depth. If the shaft is dug within the limit of time, and of the required dimensions, the commissioner of mines gives the new proprietor a certificate of protection available for twelve months. No other miner has then the right to work within a pre-arranged radius of his claim. If the conditions are not fulfilled the claim is taken back, at least, unless the proprietor can justify himself.

Does the activity displayed by these hardy pioneers remunerate them duly for the immense labour undergone in these first few months?

That is for the future to show. At present, as I have said, the greatest obstacle arises from the difficulty of transport. But the pioneers of Matabeleland firmly hope that the Mafeking railway will reach Bulawayo in three years.¹

From a material point of view, railways form one of the most active factors of civilisation; they may be compared to the arteries which carry the blood through the human body and give life to all its parts. It seems to me that the country will only realise its true value when Bulawayo is united by the projected railway to

¹ The work of this line has been forwarded by Mr. Cecil Rhodes with rare energy. The first locomotive reached Bulawayo on October 16, 1897; a few days later, on November 4, there was an inaugural festivity. *Author.*

THE OUTPOSTS OF CIVILISATION 217

Mafeking in the south and by the not less desirable extension to Beira in the east.

Another point to be determined is whether the country will fulfil its promise in the matter of the yield of auriferous quartz, which is believed to exist to a considerable extent under the surface, so much as in

NATIVES MAKING FIRE
From a photograph

the matter of the produce of the soil properly so called.

In any case, none can succeed in gaining a livelihood in these new countries but men gifted with great energy, ready to work far harder than in Europe, and able to support privations of which new colonists have in general no idea.

CHAPTER XIII

THE GOLD-MINING COUNTRY

From Bulawayo, by Matabeleland, to the Transvaal — Pretoria — Johannesburg—The Jameson Raid.

December 13th.—After passing an agreeable evening yesterday with the Commissioner of Mines, Mr. F——, we set out on the coach, which is drawn by eight pair of mules. Bulawayo soon sinks below the horizon, and we gallop over a grass country, where here and there the ruins of villages destroyed at the time of the last war are visible. The coach is driven by two drivers at break-neck speed. However, the passage of the watercourses—it is needless to say there are no bridges—has to be undertaken at a gentler pace; at certain difficult places we have to dismount, and often put our shoulders to the wheels. The drivers on the left hand hold the reins, sitting on a raised seat; the driver on the right hand is armed with an enormous two-handed whip. A little postilion of marvellous agility is now on the footboard, now running along the team, to wake up the idle or recalcitrant mules. The coach, which is of American build, is very high on its wheels; the body is ingeniously suspended on a number of superimposed springs, which, in general, prevent an upset. Like a vessel at sea, plunging and rising with the waves, it resists the inequalities—stones, holes, and

THE COACH.   *Drawn by Van Muyden*

hollows—of the track we are following. Nine places being taken inside, without counting the outside, we have our full complement. I am lucky enough to have for neighbour the first magistrate of Gazaland, who is at present on provisional service at Fort Tuli on the Transvaal frontier, as well as being a lawyer at Bulawayo.

The rest of the company is, perhaps, less agreeable, but it atones for this fault in proving a source of unending observations. The most sympathetic physiognomy is that of the pioneer, Daniel H——, an old cavalry volunteer, who served in the Zulu war, and tells us numberless anecdotes of his past life; he had, formerly, a farm in Matabeleland.

We have relays every twelve or fifteen miles; at mealtimes, which are of necessity variable, we sit down to table in the little hostelries, where we find a *cuisine* which is, above all, abundant. During the day we cross the Matoppo Hills.

These granite hills are very picturesque: they are in part formed of great heaped-up rocks of granite covered with verdure.* The last relay for to-day is at Monsianana. We shall be able to sleep there from ten p.m. to four a.m., at which hour we can resume on the coach the interrupted conversations of the night before.

December 14th.—After lunch, the character of the landscape changes; we enter the veldt, and at sunset arrive at Fort Tuli, situated on the banks of the Shashi river, at the southern extremity of the country. On our arrival, one of our companions, a very unattractive person, is forced to interrupt his journey against his will; in fact, he is attended by the police-officer. After this incident we

---

* It was here that the Matabele, a few weeks later, revolted and massacred a large number of white colonists.—*Author.*

go to sleep in the little round huts, which form the bedrooms of the inn.

December 15th.—Awakened at one a.m. by a trumpet-call, we continue our journey. We cross the Shashi river without trouble; it is broad, but now dry. Shortly afterwards we have to cross the Limpopo, the River of Crocodiles,

A ZULU WARRIOR
From a photograph

which is fairly full; the mules go down into the water bravely; it comes up to their breasts, and enters the body of the coach.

Matabeleland is bounded by the Limpopo on the south; with the right bank we reach the soil of the Boers' country, the Transvaal Republic. At sunrise one of the drivers fires on a panther, and misses. The trail is bad; it is a pleasure to watch from the top of the coach the skill of the drivers in keeping their team of ten mules going at full speed. At the posting-stations, which for the most part consist of a square, earthen stable, open at one side, and flanked by a kraal, the relays are waiting outside, ranged in line in charge of a black. On account of the simplicity of the harness, the operation of changing is finished in a few minutes. The mules, well-fed and cared for, are superbly shaped. We have uniform teams composed of bay, grey, and roan mules; their croup and their fine shape remind one of the zebra, and, like those fiery inhabitants of the open veldt, their quarters are often striped with alternating bands of light and dark.

In the course of the afternoon we sight the chain of the Zoutpansberg to the west, and Blaauwberg, or the Blue Mountains, to the east. The latter are well named; at sunset, after passing through several changes of colour, we see them turn to the most intense blue. In the distance we see some ostriches in search of their evening meal.

We reach the stage at seven p.m.; as I have remarked before, our sleeping hours are short, and we are called between eleven p.m. and midnight.

December 16th. After passing between the two chains of mountains mentioned above, we are soon galloping across the Zoutpansberg veldt. So far, with rare exceptions, we gain from the road we have pursued the impression of a vast inhabited country. We see a number of large native villages to-day; the women are working in the fields, and the young shepherds are tending the horned cattle; here and there a few farms are scattered over the grassy plain; they belong to Europeans or Boers. It is just two o'clock when we reach Pieterburg, where the afternoon rest is devoted to sleep. There is not much to see in this little town, which numbers a thousand inhabitants, who are to-day celebrating one of the victories gained by the Boers in 1838 or 1840.

December 17th.—We start at three a.m. We pass through a narrow, picturesque valley, leading from the great defile formed by the Iron Mountains. Four relays take us to Potgieters-rust, whose few white houses are hidden in luxuriant foliage, and surrounded by banana plantations. In one of these, for the first time for a long period, I am able to procure fruit—bananas, pomegranates, and, above all, excellent muscatel grapes. The country presently clears; then, during the latter half of the day, we reach the most picturesque part of the journey, the Waterberg Pass, formed by high, rocky hills, with pleasing outlines, covered with fresh verdure.

From the summit of the pass we enjoy a wide view across the plain, from which emerge conical summits more or less denuded, and which is crossed by numerous chains of mountains. Between five and six o'clock we reach another little town, Nylstroom, where we pass the night. Since this morning we have travelled one hundred miles. This is our record so far.

December 18th.—We begin our last day on the coach at two a.m. At noon we come to a wide, marshy plain, where we encounter a number of Boer waggons in difficulties. Then our light-footed team founders several times in the road, and we have to dismount to get them out again.

As we advance, so the countenance of the country changes; it becomes smiling, undulating, and brilliantly green; the farms and dwelling-houses are becoming more frequent, and at five p.m. we enter Pretoria.

I have, then, travelled the 500 miles from Bulawayo to Pretoria, the capital of the Transvaal, in six days and five nights, having passed at a gallop, behind eight or ten mules frequently changed, through the centre and south of Matabeleland and the Transvaal, almost entirely crossing the latter. This mode of travelling, which many people regard with apprehension, may be considered very comfortable after our past experiences.

Nevertheless, when the traveller finally descends from the coach, he finds himself so impregnated with dust that he needs more than one bath to resume a decent human countenance, and present himself once more among his fellows.

This coach service is very well organised, and is subsidised by the Government. There are usually two departures a week from Bulawayo for Pretoria.

December 28th.—Pretoria, joined to the south by the railway, enjoys all the advantages of civilisation. I write these lines in a room of a comfortable hotel in the Kerckplatz, a large square overlooked by a Dutch church, around which are the Government House, the post and telegraph offices, &c.; hence also runs the principal thoroughfare, Kerck-street, which contains a number of shops.

A Transvaalian, Dr. B——, the director of the museum, has rendered my stay here very agreeable by introducing me to several of the notabilities of the town. My dress-clothes being at the Cape, hundreds of miles away, I am obliged to attend these receptions in travelling, not to say hunting, dress—that is, in a short jacket, flannel waistcoat, and breeches, which does not fail to form a contrast with the smart toilets of the women and the black coats of the men. I am received most kindly, and it would take many pages to speak of all the interesting conversations I have had.

A few days before Christmas a number of Boer families

arrived in Pretoria from the surrounding farms, to take
part in the great Christian festival; fathers, mothers,
children, and servants, travelling patriarchal fashion in
their waggons, behind their teams of long-horned oxen.
They pitched their tents, or lived in their waggons, on

PRETORIA GOVERNMENT HOUSE.
From a photograph

the space surrounding the church. I attended divine
service, which was accompanied by fine singing.

A Swiss, M. S——, who came out to the Transvaal ten
years ago, invited me to spend Christmas with him at a
farm he rents nine miles out of Pretoria. I was very

kindly received. A European receives a singular impression on finding a fine Christmas-tree in the generously-decorated dining-room, and seeing out-of-doors, in a July temperature, the gardens in flower and the trees laden with fruit. We regaled ourselves with pears picked with our own hands.

During the several days I passed with M. S—— I had an opportunity of going round his farm. It is 10,000 acres in extent, of which only a hundred are irrigated. When the latter are well manured as well as irrigated, they are capable of bearing as much as twelve sacks of grain to the acre; the parts not irrigated produce two sacks only. The farm consists chiefly of pasture. The cows in this country give, on an average, a gallon of milk a day, and—a curious thing—their calves must be left with them a long time, or their milk dries up at once. The Natal cows yield about double this quantity of milk.

Fruits and European vegetables grow easily, but they spring up too quickly, and have not the same flavour as in their native countries. Apples, pears, peaches, apricots, quinces, strawberries, raspberries, &c., are gathered from November to the end of February. A hundred pounds of peas sell for half-a-crown or three shillings.

M. S——, questioned as to immigration, does not, after his long experience, recommend young Europeans to attempt agriculture in the Transvaal, still less in Matabeleland.

From the beginning of May to the end of August not a drop of rain falls, besides which locusts, white ants, hail, frost, drought, the different cattle diseases,* in particular

_{* In the beginning of 1896 the rinderpest broke out in Africa, bringing ruin, famine, and desolation in its track as far as the other side of the Zambezi. The cattle perished by the hundred thousand; they say that in Bechuanaland alone the loss amounted to 800,000 head of cattle! *Author.*}

_{Dr. Koch has recently inoculated cattle for rinderpest with perfect success. *Trans.*}

the "horse sickness," a malady peculiar to the horse, wage a desperate war against agriculture.

Dissatisfied with the results obtained by agriculture properly so called, M. S—— began some years ago a vast undertaking on his estate, the establishment of a forest of twelve hundred acres, with a thousand trees to the acre. He chose for this purpose two species of eucalyptus—the red gum, which resists frost well, the timber of which is used for railway sleepers and for use in mines, and the blue gum, which grows rapidly, but whose timber is less valued.

M. S—— cultivates several varieties of these two species. Here, in a few words, is his manner of setting to work: The seeds are obtained at a great expense from Australia. In December he sows under glass. In the middle of January the plants are thinned out to a distance of three inches from one another, and four weeks afterwards the seedlings are already three inches high. They are then potted, and then transplanted to the soil which will later on become the forest, and has been prepared to that end. At the end of a year these trees are ten or twelve feet high; next year, if circumstances have have been favourable, they are six feet taller. Five years after transplanting the trees have an average height of fifty or sixty feet; the diameter of the trunk, taken four feet from the ground, is then ten inches.

Pretoria, the capital of the Transvaal, well situated in an amphitheatre of hills, is hidden in the midst of trees, which give it a distinct individuality. No census has been taken lately; however, I have received from two official sources the following figures: the one authority making 12,000 whites and 18,000 blacks and the other 6,000 whites and 4,000 blacks. I incline to accept the latter estimate. The whites are divided into English, Dutch—a large number of whom occupy high official positions—Germans, and, finally, Boers, who form only a very insignificant minority in their own capital, for they are above all agriculturalists. The commerce of Pretoria is chiefly with the north of the country.

December 29th.—I left to-day for Johannesburg, the gold-mining town. Revolutionary plots have been afoot there latterly, and many of the inhabitants have already sent their women and children off to the Cape. The new-comers wish to have a voice in the affairs of the Transvaal.

Accompanied by the Swiss Consul, Mr. F——, of Zurich, I took the train to Johannesburg, in the centre of the Transvaal gold-mining district. We were presently rolling across wide, grassy, undulating plains, on which numerous herds were grazing. After the different modes of locomotion I have experimented with for so long, it was a real treat to feel myself once more on a train going at full speed. This line is hardly two years old, but runs many miles before reaching its destination. It crosses the line of the auriferous reefs; on all sides we see the tall chimneys of the plant employed by the companies exploiting the precious metal; an image of industry and activity.

The houses and cottages grow denser; presently we enter Park Station, Johannesburg. Mr. F—— offers me hospitality during my stay in the town.

Johannesburg is in tumult; there is a great panic to-day. The heads of families are sending their wives and children out of the way of possible danger; the trains for the South are taken by assault.

The cause of this extraordinary situation may be explained in two words: the population of the town numbers at least 80,000, of whom 75 per cent. are

JOHANNESBURG MARKET
From a photograph

"Uitlanders," and it is the latter who have made the prosperity of the country. There is no need to say that the majority of the "Uitlanders" are Anglo-Saxons. For a long time they have demanded of the Transvaal Government the right to vote, as well as certain other advantages, but the authorities of the country have systematically turned a deaf ear. As to whether they have other motives, that is not easy to say.

Be it as it may, in order to give weight to their demands, and to bring pressure to bear on the Government, they have founded the National Union, which has just issued a manifesto to the inhabitants of the Transvaal clearly enouncing their grievances, and the rights they wish to enjoy. The public speak openly of organising an armed body of volunteers; in a word, Johannesburg is on the eve of revolution.

December 30th. I have sent a letter of introduction to Mr. L—— P——, the President of the Chamber of Mines. He is also one of the leaders of the above-mentioned movement. I receive a card from him giving me permission to visit the celebrated Robinson Mine on January 2nd—if the state of the country does not force it to stop work. I present another letter to Mr. A—— W——, the director of the Transvaal Coal Trust Company, owning some coal mines to the east of the Rand, which I am anxious to see. The permission asked is at once granted, although Mr. W—— doubts if I shall be able to carry out my project on account of the coming political events. As no date is indicated on the card, I shall go at my own risk and peril to-morrow morning.

At the station, just as we were starting, I was so fortunate as to make the acquaintance of Mr. E—— W——, engineer-in-chief to the Transvaal Coal Trust Company. During the journey he gives me extremely interesting details of the auriferous basin we are crossing diagonally, in an easterly direction, to arrive at Brackpan, the most important pit worked by his company.

After lunch we descend, accompanied by an engineering expert, by a vertical shaft 300 feet in depth, to the principal gallery of the mine. It is lit by electricity; the whole of the galleries comprise a length of about twenty-five miles. The coal is extracted by gangs of blacks armed with picks, and overlooked by whites. It is then heaped up in little waggons, which are wound up to the surface. Here it is sorted by an ingenious machine, and the larger lumps are put into sacks and immediately set on the trucks of the railway abutting on the pit.

After this interesting visit the lift brings us again to the light, and we perceive that events are hastening on. The chief engineer, Mr. E—— W——, arrives at his office armed with a rifle; he is about to consult with his staff of fifty whites as to the measures to be taken to safeguard the interests of the mine, where seven or eight hundred blacks are still at work, knowing nothing of what is happening.

Delighted at having succeeded, I have just time to change the clothes I had been given for the descent, and to catch the train back to Johannesburg.

Along the track of the railway across the Rand numbers of whites and blacks are leaving the mines. There is an enormous crowd at Park Station; on leaving the station we see the first sign of hostilities, a patrol of cavalry volunteers, rifle on shoulder. The Federal escutcheon is resplendent on the principal façade of M. F——, the Swiss Consul's house; he has loaded his arms to be in readiness for everything.

The movement was perhaps concerted; to-day the town is in full revolt against the authorities of the Transvaal. A provisional government, the Reform Committee, has just been nominated; it occupies the Goldfield Office buildings in the centre of the town. A civic guard, a special police service, ambulances, and refuges for the women and children are organised. A promenade through the town offers an unforgetable spectacle. Thousands of volunteers are being enrolled and armed in the various recruiting places; the streets are full of an enthusiastic crowd which cheers them as they pass; ammunition carts are going about at full trot, as well as vehicles of all sorts, in which is to be seen the baggage of people living in the suburbs who are coming to take refuge in Johannesburg. Couriers strike sparks from the road as they gallop by. Suddenly an important piece of news spreads like lightning and electrifies the assembled thousands; a force of seven or eight hundred mounted troopers of the Chartered Company, under the orders of Dr. Jameson, has crossed the Bechuanaland frontier, invaded the Transvaal, and is advancing by forced marches to the assistance of the Johannesburg "Uitlanders."

January 1, 1896.—A splendid day. The sun is burning in all its glory, Nature is holding a festival, all is green and flourishing, the air is scented with roses: a striking contrast to the unquiet reigning in the insurgent town. Numbers of houses are shut up, and homes scattered; women and children are hastily sent away out of danger, while fathers, brothers, and husbands remain on the spot and prepare themselves for any eventualities.

Will it be possible to avoid bloodshed in Pretoria? Mr. Krüger, the President of the Transvaal Republic, has proposed an armistice. A deputation of the National Union has left this morning for the capital; will any amicable arrangement ensue therefrom? This is a question which, in the present state of the popular mind, will not take long to decide.

In the town enthusiasm is at its height. Nearly all the members of the various branches of the Anglo-Saxon race dwelling in Johannesburg, including Americans and Australians, have supported the provisional government or Reform Committee. Most of the French and Germans seem desirous to remain neutral.

Five camps of volunteers form a line of outposts outside the town, and hold the approaches. Although the people are in revolt, admirable order reigns in the streets, from which the civil police have been withdrawn and replaced by volunteer constables. Most of the shops have barricaded their fronts with planks or sheets of corrugated iron. On all sides are placards indicating the points of muster for the troops, or the places where the women, children, and destitute can find help and protection. In the public places the different corps of volunteers, distinguished by cockades of various colours, are being drilled by men who seem to me to have the look of ex-officers or non-coms. They are all armed with an excellent magazine rifle.

There is a great stationary crowd in front of the offices of the provisional government; the doors are guarded by a line of twelve sentries, ranged in two ranks, their rifles grounded. Numbers of messengers, galloping at full speed, are bringing news from without or going in search of orders. Various rumours are in circulation as to the approach of Jameson's force, which is waited for impatiently.

At the Rand Club we learn of a railway accident which took place on the line joining the Transvaal with Natal, which has only been opened a few days. Forty-three killed and a number wounded; the train was full of women and children escaping from the revolution.

In the course of the afternoon the Reform Committee announces publicly that the Government of the South

African Republic has accepted the offer of mediation by Sir Hercules Robinson, the English High Commissioner. He will leave the Cape instantly, and arrive at Pretoria in three days' time—on Saturday next.

January 2nd.—After a day passed in alternate hope and anxiety, the town has learned, to its consternation, that Jameson's troop has been defeated fifteen miles out of Johannesburg.

While recognising that this force committed an act contrary to international law by invading a neighbouring state during a time of peace, it would be impossible not to insist—as, indeed, many of the Boers themselves have done—on the bravery of this handful of men who, in three days and nights, almost without sleep, with scarcely time to eat, have accomplished a forced march of one hundred and eighty miles, in one day making a distance of ninety miles.

Following their usual tactics, the Boers, who are splendid shots, awaited them in a position where all the advantages were theirs. Jameson's troopers lost a seventh or eighth of their effective force—about twenty-four killed and wounded—and surrendered only at the last extremity.

Here is a brief account of the raid given by a man who accompanied the column. I transcribe it from a local paper:—

"It was on the night of December 30–31, between eleven and midnight, and on this side of Krügersdorp, that the first body of Boers tried to stop us. We were on a hill, and the Boers opened fire on us. We cleared the ground with the Maxims and resumed our march.

"We had plenty of provisions, but no time to eat or sleep. After crossing the Transvaal frontier, we had only one hour's sleep, which was after we had dispersed the

Boers in the first engagement I have mentioned. The rest of the time we rode.

"Early on the morning of December 31st we fired a few shots from the field-guns, as the Boers were advancing from the direction of Krügersdorp. At eleven a.m. we were able to eat and rest a little; at one p.m. we resumed our march, always on this side of Krügersdorp. Near Krügersdorp the Boers were entrenched in a mine, of which they had occupied the upper works. We bombarded their position with our field-pieces; the firing continued all night, and the attacks succeeded one another until the morning of January 1st. At this moment our camp had just been formed, and the order to offsaddle had not yet been given, when we were overwhelmed by the Boer fire.

"The last engagement took place not far from Dornkop, where the Boers held a commanding position. A detachment of our column was ordered to go forward with a Maxim and a field-gun; when they had done so they found that the Boers held a second position beyond the first, and our main column was presently caught between their two fires. This was the only place where we could force a passage; but it was a dangerous operation."

The provisional government or Reform Committee issued on January 3rd the two following proclamations:—

1. "On the part of Her Majesty's representative to the Secretary of the Reform Committee, Johannesburg.

"At the request of the deputation which you have sent to me, I have put myself in communication with His Honour the President of the Transvaal, and he has given me assurance that, pending the arrival of the High Commissioner, who has left the Cape this evening, Johannesburg shall not be invaded by the Boers, on the condition that the people do not infringe the laws or commit any act hostile to the Government.

"(Signed), J. A. DE WET,
"Her Majesty's chargé d'affaires."

2. Reform Committee Notice: "The Committee recognises that the present position of Dr. Jameson is one of extreme gravity, and that all aggressive action on the part of the said Committee must seriously complicate that position. Sir Hercules Robinson, the High Commissioner of Her Majesty Queen Victoria, will arrive at Pretoria on the coming Saturday. The Committee hopes that the people of Johannesburg will understand the absolute necessity of maintaining order.

"The Government of the Transvaal has given assurance that its forces will not march against Johannesburg; it also adds that it will give no pretext for a conflict. Nevertheless, the Committee have taken necessary precautions in all that concerns the public safety.

"By order of the Committee,
"(Signed), The Secretary,
"J. PERCY FITZPATRICK."[*]

Immediately after the battle of Dornkop, the Boers led Jameson and his men prisoners to Pretoria. The spoils of war include eight Maxims and three field-guns of 2·9 in. calibre.[†]

The Boers are concentrating from all parts of the country. The population of Johannesburg is less demonstrative than on the preceding days. Although the town has lost nothing of its warlike aspect, and the volunteers energetically continue their drill, the arrival of

---

[*] These documents, and the newspaper extract, are re-translated from Captain Bertrand's French. *Trans.*

[†] Capt Bertrand gives the calibre as 0·075 m.—probably 3·0 in. *Trans.*

the High Commissioner in Pretoria is to-day (Saturday) awaited with impatience.

Johannesburg is already surrounded at some distance by a cordon of several thousand Boers, but it is foreseen that no event of importance can take place before the day after to-morrow, for the Boers, to their credit be it said, never put themselves in the field on a Sunday, nor does President Krüger allow affairs of state to be undertaken on that day under any pretext.

On January 5th we went as far as the volunteer camp defending the north of the town. The men are billeted in an orphanage. It is a picturesque encampment; here the horses are picketed, there the tents are pitched, and on all sides we see groups of volunteers variously accoutred. They belong to all different classes of society. We drive in the carriage as far as the vicinity where the first advance-guards of the Boers should be. Now as always, according to their customary tactics, they are invisible; we see nothing but horses peacefully grazing. This lovely sunny morning, amid the smiling countryside, evokes no ideas but those of peace.

January 6th.—This evening the Reform Committee received from Pretoria, through Her Majesty's chargé d'affaires, the following advice from the Transvaal Government: " The people of Johannesburg must first of all lay down their arms, before their grievances can be discussed. On this condition only Jameson and his force will be placed in the hands of the Imperial authorities to be tried. The reply to this ultimatum must be given within twenty-four hours—by four p.m. on Tuesday.

The Reform Committee ended by accepting this proposition.

January 7th.—The English chargé d'affaires in the

Transvaal, Sir Jacobus de Wet, arrived in Johannesburg. In the presence of 7,000 men he delivered an eloquent speech, by which he prevailed upon every one to accept the proposition of the Government in order to save the life of Jameson, and prevent a conflict which might have terrible consequences.

The arms were laid down. A movement of evident relief was visible among the inhabitants. The shops opened their fronts, peaceable folk once more went about their business, and little by little the town resumed its ordinary aspect. The flag of the Convention of Geneva, a red cross on a white ground, the familiar emblem of peace and charity, has been well in evidence these last few days in Johannesburg, for numerous ambulances were organised, and it still floats proudly above the fine hospital which rises above the town.

The English High Commissioner, Sir Hercules Robinson, must have given a sigh of relief when the news of the disarmament reached him. The demands of the Uitlanders can be discussed at leisure with President Krüger. One of the principal grievances is that the existing laws give them no hope of acquiring the right to vote, either now or in the future.

All impartial observers cannot do otherwise than testify to the perfect order that reigned in the town during the time of revolution. The influx of thousands of white and black miners at such a critical time, to say nothing of the vagabonds which are never lacking in a town of 24,000 inhabitants, would at first sight seem a sufficient cause of anxiety. But they knew that any attempt at disorder would be repressed with the utmost energy by a population who on this point would not have hesitated.

January 9th.—Quiet being more or less established

after this troublesome period, I can at last fulfil a desire I have long entertained to visit the celebrated Robinson gold-mine. To describe it would take pages; I must content myself with a few lines.

Accompanied by a miner, we seat ourselves in a truck which takes us by an inclined plane to the lowest gallery. The depth of this gallery is 1,100 feet horizontally and 700 vertically. We distinguish plainly the three reefs of auriferous quartz—the South Reef, the Main Reef Leader, and the Main Reef.

These are the processes undergone by the precious metal from the time when it is dragged from the bowels of the earth to the moment of its conversion into ingots.

The "banket," an auriferous conglomerate, is blasted with dynamite, and loaded on iron "skips" or trollies. After being drawn to the mouth of the shaft it is tipped into a receptacle or reservoir in which the process of sorting is undergone, and after the barren rock has been removed the conglomerate goes to the crushing-machine, which brays it into pieces about the size of a pea. It is then shot into bins at the bottom of which are automatic doors, and little railed waggons convey it to the stamping-battery.

The stamps are grouped by fives, and there are twenty-four of these groups in the battery. When the crushed "banket" has been stamped into a very fine powder it passes through a sieve and runs on to a table of pure copper covered with mercury, with which the particles of gold amalgamate. The copper pans or tables are cleared once or twice a day, according to the richness of the dust, and the amalgam is distilled over from retorts. The mercury is vapourised and condensed with cold water; the gold is then smelted with borax in graphite crucibles, and run into ingots.

The sludge which now trickles off the copper trays

consists of sand, of varying degrees of fineness, in suspension in water, and contains gold in a non-amalgamable form, probably in combination with pyrites, which is often found in gold-bearing stuffs. To separate the pyrites, and consequently the gold, the sludge passes through concentrators which separate it into two products: firstly, a rather small percentage (about 5 per cent.) of concentrated sludge which contains all the pyrites, and secondly, a mixture of sands of various kinds.

The former product contains gold in very large proportions; it is grilled in long ovens, and thus converted into oxide of iron containing gold. This oxidised product is then treated with chlorine, which combines with 98 per cent. of the gold contained in the concentrated product.

The sand, or "tailings," also contains a certain percentage of gold, and is treated with a solution of cyanide of potassium; the cyanide dissolves the gold, which is then precipitated by shavings of metallic zinc.

The resultant mixture of zinc and gold, or "cyanite slime," is treated with sulphuric acid, which dissolves the greater part of the zinc; the remaining product is dried, grilled, and smelted with borax in graphite crucibles, as before, and run into ingots.

I am indebted for this description to one of the chief engineers of the Witwatersrand; I will conclude it by saying that the "Robinson" has an average staff of 350 whites and over 1,000 blacks.

January 10th.—The town continues calm, although fifty-six members of the defunct Reform Committee have been arrested and taken to Pretoria, where they are to be tried. Besides this, for the last two or three days no one has been allowed to enter or leave Johannesburg by rail without a written permit from the Traansvaal Government. Here are a few notes on the subject of this government taken from the "Official Handbook of the Cape":

The President of the Transvaal Republic, at present Mr. S. J. P. Krüger, is elected by a majority of burghers. He has charge of the executive, for which he is responsible to the Volksraad or Houses of Parlia-

PRESIDENT KRUGER'S RESIDENCE AT PRETORIA
From a photograph

ment. He proposes the laws which seem to him necessary, or which have been suggested to him by the burghers; he must visit each year all the towns of the Republic, and he cannot absent himself from the country without the consent of the Houses.

The President exercises his power conjointly with the Executive Council, which consists of the Commander-in-chief, General J. P. Joubert, the latter being elected by the people for ten years; two members chosen by the Volksraad for two years, and the Secretary of State elected by the Volksraad for four years. The Superintendent of Native Affairs and the Keeper of the Minutes are by right members of the Council. The President may also invite the different heads of departments to be present in Council, and to vote in any matters concerning their respective departments.

The President of the Republic and the members of the Executive Council have seats in both Houses, but have no vote there.

Each House consists of twenty-four burghers of at least thirty years of age, property-owners, and members of the Protestant Church.

The resolutions passed by the Lower House must be notified to the President and to the Upper House within forty-eight hours. The Upper House may, on its own initiative or on the advice of the President, revise, confirm, or reject the decisions of the Lower House.

The official language is Dutch.

I may add that the President of the Republic receives an annual emolument of £8,000. He receives an additional income of £400 per annum, destined in part to pay for the coffee which he offers to persons received at the morning audience, between six and eight, or in the evening. I am sorry that political circumstances prevented me from fulfilling my intention of being presented to the President during my visit to Pretoria.

Seventy-five per cent. of the population of the Transvaal, which amounts to several hundreds of thousands, are Uitlanders. They are, in general, active, enterprising, and intelligent people. At present, as we have already seen, they are entirely excluded from the affairs of the country. Nevertheless, Johannesburg, the "golden city," which was so lately on the brink of being smitten with fire and blood, owes its existence to them. It is in fact these Uitlanders who have discovered and exploited this gold-bearing district; and as I was told by one of the first Europeans who arrived in these parts, the site on which the well-built town of Johannesburg stands to-day, was ten years ago a vast plain.

On the other hand the Boers, perhaps with reason, fear that the Transvaal may lose its independence, when strangers can easily attain the dignity of burghers—that is to say, to the condition of citizens.

January 13th.—I leave Johannesburg.

CHAPTER XIV

THE GARDEN OF SOUTH AFRICA—THE RETURN

From Johannesburg to Durban—East London—Port Elizabeth—The Cape—Return to Europe.

AFTER a night passed on the train I woke at the frontier of Natal on January 14th. This new line, joining Johannesburg to Natal on the Indian Ocean, was inaugurated only a few days ago. We cross various ramifications of the chain of the Drakensberg. Here and there we catch glimpses of the surrounding country, which is largely broken and wooded. In the course of the forenoon we pass seven trucks laden with the *débris* of the train I spoke of while at Johannesburg, which ran off the rails on December 31st not far from Glencoe Junction, when forty people were killed or wounded.

Late in the evening we arrive in Durban, the principal seaport of the colony. I go to visit one of my cousins, M. C. M——, a native of Geneva, an ex-officer in the English navy, who several years ago established a tea plantation in the province of Victoria. To reach it I have to go by way of the North Coast Railway, which crosses many lovely hills and valleys, where the eye is charmed by the abundance of flowers, by plantations of sugar and other growths, as far as the terminus, the little town of Verulam. There in a few

VIEW OF DURBAN
From a photograph

hours a two-wheeled coach, drawn by six horses, takes the traveller over hill and vale to Stanger. Here I bestride a pony which is sent to meet me, and a ride of nine or ten miles through a mountainous, wooded country soon takes me to Merindol, the estate in question. A warm welcome awaits me.

M. M— established the estate, which is admirably situated, six years ago. It stretches over three hills. The house, surrounded by bananas, eucalyptus, bamboos, and various other trees, overlooks the surrounding country. From the verandah, overgrown with honeysuckle and roses, the horizon stretches twelve miles eastward to the Indian Ocean, just visible to the naked eye.

Tea-planting was begun in Natal in 1877, when a few acres were planted experimentally. To-day the country contains 3,000 acres of tea-plants in prime condition, which produce annually a million pounds of tea. Natal tea is spreading rapidly through the South African and English markets. It has been compared favourably with the tea of other countries. The climate and the nature of the soil produce a tea less strong and acrid than that of India or Ceylon, which has yet a body and a bouquet which permit of its consumption unblended with other teas.

The culture of tea must be undertaken with great care. After a favourable site has been found for the future plantation the soil is tilled and harrowed, and then marked out in lines from four feet six inches to five feet six inches apart. Stakes are driven into these lines every four or five feet; holes a foot in depth are dug near each stake, and are filled with finely reduced earth; and the young tea-plants, which have been grown from seed and kept under cover for some weeks, are then transplanted in moist weather. The future plantation must be very carefully overseen, and drained by open trenches. Avenues of trees, often bananas, are planted to protect the tea-plants from the wind.

After two years the young plants are three or four feet high; at this period they are polled at a height of three feet from the ground, in order to increase their growth and facilitate picking.

The first picking takes place in the course of the fourth year, when the rains are beginning to fall. In the follow-

A PLANTER'S HOUSE
From a photograph

ing years the pickings may be repeated every ten days or fortnight during the rainy season, from the end of September to the end of May. On several occasions we were present at the pickings. It is a charming sight, that of the straight rows of beautiful deep-green shrubs, enclosed by long avenues of bananas with bright, gracefully drooping leaves. Against this background of foliage stand out the figures of the Hindoo coolies, dressed in brightly-coloured stuffs, rapidly filling their linen bags with the tender leaves under the vigilant supervision of the "sirdar." They merely pinch off the tips of the young shoots, thus plucking four or five leaves at a time.

A tea plantation in full swing produces 2,000 lbs. to 2,400 lbs. of green leaves per acre per annum. Four pounds of green leaves are considered equivalent to one pound of prepared tea.

A good workman can pick eighty to a hundred pounds of tea daily; the average is fifty pounds.

To-day there are five tea manufacturers in this district (Kearsney), to whom many of the planters send their pickings of green leaves twice a day. We inspected in one of these factories the various extremely delicate operations through which the leaves must pass before reaching their final state, when they are ready to be infused to give the excellent beverage we enjoy every day.

After each sack has been weighed and marked in the presence of the owner, the leaves, when they have reached the manufacturer, are first of all spread out on sheet-iron drying-trays, over which flows a current of hot air. Here they wither in a maximum period of twenty hours. They are then poured into the steam rolling-machine through an opening in the centre of the top rolling-plate. This ingenious machine consists of two parallel plates, having a circular motion, like that of two gigantic hands rubbing their palms together, and it may be said to fulfil a similar purpose. The pressed and rolled leaves are then taken out in a mass, and are usually placed in a covered chest for about half-an-hour; they must be carefully watched during this time, in order to let them proceed to the necessary degree of fermentation. After this fermentation the leaves acquire a deep rich, warm colour, besides their peculiar bouquet.

HINDOO COOLIES PICKING TEA
Drawn by Baader, from a photograph

One of the last operations consists in drying the tea in the " Down-Draught Sirocco " drying machine. The hot air is introduced from above into an iron case containing numerous drawers. The fermented tea is first placed in the lowest drawer, and gradually removed, drawer by drawer, to the highest, in which the operation of drying comes to an end. We have then the dried and prepared tea before our eyes. By means of another machine it is assorted into three different qualities; it is then made into packets and is ready for transport.

The Hindoo coolies who work in these plantations are largely dependent on the Natal Government, and it is to the " Protector," resident in Durban, that the planters address themselves when in need of their services.

The coolies, who are recruited principally in the provinces of Madras and Calcutta, sign an engagement to serve for five years under the Government. When their time has expired they can re-engage themselves for the same period, but year by year only, as the Government does not wish them to become permanent inhabitants in the country. The passage both ways is paid by the Government. They receive a fixed wage from the planter, and also an allotment on his estate, on which they establish their huts and gardens. The planter also furnishes them with provisions, of which the quantity and quality are fixed in advance. In case of illness the coolies are visited by doctors and treated free of charge in special hospitals.

The coolie who has complaints to make can apply to the local magistrate or await the periodical inspection of the Protector or his agents. The Protector has also the right to inspect the books, which every planter has to keep day by day, in which the work and payment of the coolies are registered, and also the sick-roll, the latter being to witness to the visits of the doctor. The planter

cannot evict the coolies from his property during the
period of his contract, but he has the right of inflicting
certain punishments, and in the event of a serious case
refers to the magistrate.

My quiet stay in my cousin's house, where the hospitality is so cordial, amidst this country so well endowed
both by nature and climate, offers a great contrast to the
days passed recently in Johannesburg in full revolution.

It is summer with us; at this altitude (1,100 feet, the
temperature has been by no means excessive hitherto, as
we benefit by refreshing sea-breezes. The ananas, like

THE MERINDOL RIVER, NATAL.
From a photograph

great golden globes, are ripe now, and we go out to pick
them for breakfast. Millions of locusts have just invaded
Natal. Their innumerable legions are almost everywhere,
and are working great havoc. Happily—it is a curious
thing—they do not attack the tea-tree.

To drive them away great fires are lit through the
country, and the coolies run about the various plantations
making as much noise as possible.

We enjoyed recently, from the summit of Red Hill, a

splendid view of the surrounding country: a veritable maze of tree-clad hills and green valleys, bounded on the east by the Indian Ocean, and to the north by the chain of high mountains which run through Zululand, the frontier of which we can see at a distance of some twelve miles. The Zulus are reputed to be the most valiant fighting-men of South Africa.

January 19*th.*—To-day, Sunday, my cousin and I have been invited to visit the Hon. J. Liege-Huet, M.P., at his beautiful estate of Kearsney. He was one of the initiators of tea-culture in this country, and is to-day the most considerable planter in Natal. Before the midday meal Mr. Liege-Huet himself held a religious service, simple and moving, in the little chapel built on his grounds. When I see him afterwards surrounded by his family at table a lively image of the patriarchal life suddenly springs up in my mind. Assuredly it is the men of his stamp that make the strength and greatness of English colonisation.

January 23*rd.*—During this last day at Merindol a *mamba*, a particularly venomous snake, was killed on a tree near the house.

The locusts cover the country; they form a living carpet, and the beautiful leaves of the banana-trees are devoured in the twinkling of an eye. The leafage of a neighbouring field of mealies, fifty acres in extent, has vanished in the same way.

Mr. Liege-Huet offers me his hospitality again for the last evening we shall be able to pass together. His property is nearer to Stanger, where the Verulam coach passes in the early morning.

January 24*th.*—Just as we are getting into our saddles

to meet the coach we learn that the available places have
been engaged by the soldiers of the garrison at Exhowe,
a few miles away on the frontier of Zululand. As soldiers
always have the precedence of civilians we can only
accept the state of affairs. I do not let myself be
discouraged by so little, which is well, for on reaching
Stanger a resident lets me a light trap and a powerful
horse. Taking up the reins I soon accomplish the
twenty-eight miles to Verulam—the railway terminus—
and arrive in time to take the afternoon train.

A letter Mr. Liege-Huet gave me on my departure
authorises me to visit *en route* the most important
refinery in the country, the Natal Central Sugar
Company Factory. I soon have it in view, and get out
at the station. The principal building of the refinery is
surmounted by a chimney ninety feet high.

The sugar-cane is carried by little waggons to the rolls,
a powerful machine which give it two crushings to extract
all the sugar, while the " baagas"—fibrous parts of the
cane—is rejected at the other end, and is dried to serve as
fuel. At the moment of crushing a perfect cascade of
syrup pours into the large vats. The greenish, watery
fluid is then boiled in cauldrons. After the colouring
principles have been carried off by sulphuric acid vapour,
it is passed through clarifiers which remove its impurities.
Its natural acidity is corrected with lime.

The syrup, having been filtered afresh, arrives succes-
sively at the " triple-action machine," where the water is
evaporated, and at the vacuum pans, where the sugar
crystallises. It has to be cooled before being thrown into
one of the sixteen centrifugal separators, which remove
the molasses. We have then a fine white sugar of the first
quality; it is dried, and is then ready for market. The
molasses remaining over is boiled again and again in the
centrifugal separators; the result is a second quality of

A PRETTY CORNER, NEAR KEARSNEY, NATAL.
From a photograph

sugar. The same process repeated gives a third quality of sugar. The residue is distilled and used as compost.

January 25th.—To reach the dwelling-house of the obliging director of this flourishing industrial enterprise, I have to skirt numerous fields of sugar-cane. The director kindly kept me at his house, and only allowed me to take my departure this morning, not without having given me numerous details of the culture and yield of the cane.

To-day the plantations of sugar-cane in the colony of Natal cover a superficies of 20,000 acres, or thirty-one square miles, which yields an annual crop of 20,000 tons, or nearly 45,000,000 lbs. of sugar. Of this total, the Natal Central Sugar Company cultivates 5,000 acres, producing 4,000 tons, or nearly 10,000,000 lbs. of sugar annually.

Durban, with its population of 30,000, is not merely the port of Natal, but also a commercial centre of great importance, and the prettiest town in this part of Africa. It is well built, and extremely clean. The best means of seeing it is to enter one of the numerous little vehicles drawn by runners, which are incessantly going to and fro. These are the means of locomotion most employed here, and remind one of the Japanese jinrikshas.

No one should forget to see the market, which gives one some idea of the richness and variety of the fruits grown in this happy country. According to the season, one finds various European fruits among the native bananas, ananas, naatjes, mandarines, citrons, oranges, mangoes, and guavas.

The town stretches along the bay, and rises in stages up the flanks of Berea hill, where the most charming houses hide themselves amid the trees and flowers of the tropics. From the Berea the view is beautiful, the bay is like a tranquil lake, and is joined to the sea by a channel which

DURBAN "RICKSHAWS." *From a photograph*

leaves the base of a cliff covered with verdure, at the extremity of which is a lighthouse. Beyond is the deep blue of the Indian Ocean. The waves that ruffle its surface seem to sprinkle it with silver. A number of large vessels are gently heaving at anchor.

Durban does credit to Natal, which is one of the most favoured English colonies of South Africa. Vasco da Gama discovered this country on Christmas Day, 1497; he christened it *Terra Natalis*. Its superficies is equal to that of England and Wales together; it is inhabited by 15,000 English, Dutch, and Germans, 40,000 Hindoo coolies, and 450,000 to 500,000 blacks.*

Since July 23, 1893, Natal has been a self-governing colony, with a government of two Houses of Parliament.

January 26th.—At sea! What a delight to breathe the sweet salt wind at sea!

There is no want of subjects of interest on the *Rosslyn Castle*, the steamer on which I embark for Cape Town, where I have a lot of baggage to recover as well as other formalities to go through. We have among the passengers ninety of Jameson's men who took part in the recent invasion of the Transvaal, including three officers, prisoners on parole under the charge of our captain. They will land at the different ports. These troopers, who count among them several members of good English families, seem strong and determined men. They are accoutred in the most incongruous fashions, for they lost nearly everything on the battlefield. Some, however, still wear the smart uniform of their regiment, the jacket and riding breeches of very light velvet cord. For headgear they wear the wide-brimmed felt rakishly turned up at the left side. They have undergone a good deal, but

* These figures were given before Zululand was annexed to Natal. *Author.*

they congratulate themselves on the manner in which the Boers treated them during their captivity in Pretoria.

One of them shows me a bullet which came out at his back after passing through his lungs. Happily for him it was fired from the new Lee-Metford rifle. These rifles of small calibre would seem, in the light of recent experiences, to be less murderous than the old ones. Their projectory force is so high that the bullet, which is very small in diameter and very long, will pass through flesh without lacerating it, and without breaking the bones.

EAST LONDON FROM THE SEA
From a photograph

A few hours after sailing we have in sight the rugged and mountainous coast of Pondoland, one of England's recent acquisitions. In particular we notice the picturesque mouth of the River St. John (Umzimburo), which flows into the sea between high tree-clad cliffs.

This afternoon I witnessed a characteristic incident: a Boer commandant and a group of officers who took part in the Jameson Raid were seated fraternally on the after-deck, and courteously discussing the mistakes in tactics committed on either side at the time of the last war.

January 27th.—We stop early in the day near East London, on the banks of the River Buffalo. The town stands out clearly, with its red-roofed houses prettily scattered over the sides of the hill. The steamers are obliged to keep some distance from the shore. The bar of East London has a bad reputation, and passengers wishing to land are transferred to a tug by means of a great closed basket hoisted by steam, an operation which is not facilitated by the rough sea.

The waves are running very high as we cross the bar, and the floating *débris* proves that wrecks are not rare. We ascend the Buffalo for a distance of a mile or two, and are quickly in East London, the third port of Cape Colony, a well-built town, with very wide streets, bordered with large houses of one story. The inaccessible beach to the east of the town, which consists of sand as white as snow, on which the waves of the Indian Ocean come to perish, is superb.

January 28th.—The *Rosslyn Castle* has taken in a large consignment of bales of wool. We go out to sea again in the evening.

January 29th.—In the morning we reach Port Elizabeth, which is far from presenting the seductive aspect of East London, although it is well situated on the north-west of the Gulf of Algoa. There is good anchorage, sheltered from the winds; the steamer has to complete its cargo here, and we must remain here for some days. One of the passengers, Mr. G. R. Halkett, a Londoner, the political correspondent of the *Pall Mall Gazette*, and the most agreeable of men, from whom every one may be sure of learning something of interest, engages me to accom-

HOW ONE LANDS AT EAST LONDON AND PORT ELIZABETH
From a photograph

pany him to the Zuurberg. We are soon landed on a
jetty, the number of steam-engines on which indicate the
activity of the town, and arrive in Main Street (at the
end of which is the Town Hall), adorned with a monu-
mental fountain in the form of an obelisk, as well as a
large covered market where ostrich feathers are sold every
week.

The railway takes us in a few hours to Coerney, towards
the north. We arrive in pitch darkness, and find refuge
in the one small hotel of the place.

There are many ostrich farms in the neighbourhood.
Next day we see a number of these enormous birds.
Although the ostrich inhabits Africa exclusively, its
beautiful feathers have been sought after in all times, and
by all the nations of the earth. The English especially
have valued them since the time when the Black Prince,
having killed the King of Bohemia at the battle of
Crecy in 1346, carried away the ostrich feathers which
soared above the helmet of the vanquished monarch, and
placed them on his own. Since then the three ostrich
feathers have always figured on the arms of the Prince of
Wales.

In 1860 the wild ostriches, which, of course, were
hunted, seemed fated to disappear little by little. Then
the idea struck some of the colonists to domesticate and
breed them, and thus obtain, thanks to their plumage, a
permanent source of revenue. In 1865 there were 80
domesticated ostriches in Cape Colony and the neighbouring
parts, while the last census, that of 1891, gave a total of
154,880. This enormous production has lowered the prices
considerably; in fact, the census of 1882 gives us a crop
of 253,954 lbs. of feathers, representing a value of
£1,080,000; whilst that of 1891 gives a yield of 257,027
lbs. of feathers, which were not valued at more than
£520,000.

January 30th.—In the middle of the afternoon we set out in a pair-horse cart, driven by a negro, for the neck of the Zuurberg. We presently cross one of the farms mentioned before, where we pass numbers of ostriches, black, white, and grey. Their bodies, seen closely, give one the idea of great defensive power. The muscular feet must be formidable weapons. The long neck is surmounted with a very small head. Ostrich chicks, already the size of a goose, covered with light down, walk solemnly around their parents.

We soon reach the flank of the mountain, which is covered with beautiful foliage, itself covered with lovely climbing plants, whose thousands of blue flowers are shaped like jasmine blossoms. Here and there we still see groups of palms and castor-oil bushes. We find several fine views to admire; on reaching the summit of the range we command a view of all the wide country stretching out to the Indian Ocean.

The proprietor of the Zuurberg Pass Hotel, Mr. S. P. B——, is a naturalist. Amongst other curiosities he shows us the eggs of the *Achatina Zebra*, a great land-snail, which may reach a length of seven or eight inches.

The chain of mountains on which we are separates us from the plain of the Karroo, which is about eighteen miles away; if we followed the road before us we should arrive at Kimberley. At this altitude, 2,300 feet, the mountains are bare of tall trees, but are covered with fine grass, their configuration recalling that of the Scottish moors.

February 1st.—We return to a nautical life on board the *Rosslyn Castle*. Port Elizabeth soon disappears on the horizon. It is called, with reference to its extensive commerce, the Liverpool of South Africa.

The sea is favourable. On February 2nd we anchor not far from Mussel Bay, an excellent port, having shelter from the east winds, halfway between Cape Town and its energetic rival, Port Elizabeth. On the night of February 3rd we double Cape Agulhao, the southern extremity of the Dark Continent. As every one knows, it is washed both by the waters of the Atlantic and the Indian Ocean, being in 20° E. longitude.

In the morning, well out at sea, we pass the Cape of Good Hope, immortalised in the "Lusiades" by the Portuguese poet, Camoëns. A few hours later the beautiful mountains of the Lion's Head, the Table, and the Devil's Peak, at whose feet Cape Town lies, are in sight, and I find myself once more in the town I left in April, 1895.

The Cape, February 3rd–13th.—While putting my affairs in order I profited by my stay in the Cape to undertake certain things I was forced to neglect on my arrival last year; for example, a visit to the wine districts.

One day I went to Constantia to see the vineyards, which are situated near the coast on the slopes of the Table Mountain. Contrary to what is usual elsewhere I was surprised to see that each vine, without the support of any prop, formed a little well laden bush two or three feet in height. I could already pick an excellent red muscatel; the grape-harvest will begin in a fortnight, at the end of February.

I may remark that the Cape colonists, thanks to their immense vineyards, are among the most important wine producers of the whole world.

The phylloxera has made serious ravages here, although energetic measures were taken to contend against it.

It is interesting to note that those vineyards situated near the coast, like this I have just visited, have suffered little from the formidable insect, as it is driven into the

THE QUAYS, CAPE TOWN
Drawn by Taylor, from a photograph

interior of the country by the extremely violent winds blowing from the sea.

Another day I visit the Museum, which is remarkably well arranged. It is worth seeing, if only to admire the splendid specimens of the African fauna fallen to the rifle of Mr. Selous, the traveller so well known in these parts.

The director told me Reid, when last here, offered the Museum the fine collection of butterflies he had got together with so many pains and so much perseverance during our journey.

February 12th.—I ought still to mention " Groote Schuur," the splendid estate of the Premier of the Cape ; Sea Point, the picturesque promenade along the shore, and many other particulars of this interesting country. But no! For here in the roads is the *Mexican* of the Union line, a steamer of 4,600 tons, on which I am about to embark.

February 13th-28th.—What a satisfaction it is, while breathing with delight the tonic sea-smell, and enjoying the varied sights of the ocean, to be able to say that the end proposed at the beginning of our bygone expedition has been attained!

* * * *

It is turned, the last page of this moving chapter, whose memory will remain engraven in the depth of my soul.

Here on board a living tie still binds me to this African soil, which, once known, can never be forgotten, in spite of all. On this vessel, which is bearing me to the fogs of the North, I meet once more with zebras, monkeys, and birds of all kinds; unhappy captives which are going far from their sunny country to people the zoological gardens of Europe. Often I go to see them, and bewail their fate. No more will they mix with those brilliant squadrons

which, at a frantic gallop, cross the wastes of those
immense solitudes. A narrow cage with rigid bars replaces the splendours of the virgin forest for these. And
they will never again beat their wings under the great
azure vault of the African sky.

March 1st.—Everybody is on the deck! The light of
Ushant, on the coast of Brittany, is in sight. And with
the appearance of that light in the night we salute old
Europe.

March 2nd.—We land at Southampton.

I do not know how better to end this book than once more to testify to M. Coillard, the venerable founder of the Zambezi Mission, as well as to his colleagues, my high esteem for the admirable work of Christian civilisation they have undertaken in the kingdom of the Barotsi.

I have also to thank the missionaries of the Zambezi for their cordial welcome, to assure them of my sentiments of friendship, and of the kindly memories I shall retain of them.

APPENDICES

APPENDIX I

Here, to sum up, are some general notes of the kingdom of the Barotsi, as yet so little known. I owe much of my information to the great kindness of the Zambezi Missionaries; other notes are the result of my own personal observation.

THE Barotsi, or Marotsi, the sovereign tribe, came from the southern extremity of Africa. They know neither the period nor the starting-point of their migration. M. Coillard, the well-known missionary explorer, is of opinion that they came from the Bonyai, a territory bordering on Matabeleland.

In 1823 the Makololo left the Lesuto;[*] they advanced little by little northwards, making war upon the Bechuanas, the Matabele, and other peoples. In 1840 they crossed the Zambezi and conquered the Barotsi, who were already in occupation of the country and were subject to the Makololo. The domination of the Makololo was cruel; the chiefs struggled among themselves, and the vanquished tribes resolved to revolt.

In 1864 the Barotsi revolted, having at their head Sepopa, one of the numerous sons of King Moramboa, who had been dethroned by the Makololo. Pushed to extremities by the tyranny of King Sepopa, the Barotsi killed him in 1877, and his nephew Nguana-Wina rose to power in his place. He abused it to such an extent that he was obliged to take flight after a reign of eight or ten months; Lewanika, nephew to Sepopa, was then proclaimed king. After a revolution and a counter revolution, Lewanika has managed, since 1885, to establish himself securely in power.

Since the time of their arrival in the country the Barotsi, a

* Basutoland. *Trans.*

superior race, have been established in the Borotsi plain, which extends from the village of Nejulona in the north to that of Seoma in the south, and also in the Borotsi gorges, that is to say, the country between Seoma on the north and the rapids of Katima-Molilo on the south. Little by little they subjected the surrounding tribes, to the number, to-day, of twenty-five or thirty. I will mention, among others :—

Tribes.

The Matotela, who inhabit the inferior basin of the Lumbi, Njoko, and Loanja rivers. They are workers in wood and iron, and also husbandmen (principally the Matotela of the Njoko, who raise cattle).

The Masubia, fishermen and boatmen. Their territory runs from Sekhosi to a point above Kazungula, and comprises the triangle formed by the Zambezi and the Linyanti.

The Batoka dwell to the east of Kazungula, and extends northwards as far as the Umgwezi river. They are hunters and agriculturalists, possessing few large cattle, but many sheep and goats.

The Mankoya encamp in the upper basins of the Machili, Njoko, and Lumbi rivers. They are almost solely hunters, living on the fruits of the forests when their arrows fail to procure game.

The Mashukulumbwe occupy the country to the east of the Mankoya, the north-eastern portion of Borotsiland. They also dwell on the banks of the Kafukwe river; they are husbandmen and breeders of horned cattle.

The Mambunda, who are given to medicine and sorcery, are grouped in different parts of the country.

The Makwenga live along the River Lui, as far up as Sefula. They work in iron and possess cattle.

These various peoples often emigrate in companies, and are distributed throughout the country.*

Superficies and Frontiers.

The square mileage of the kingdom of the Barotsi is probably greater than that of France.

Its northern frontier, which is unknown, probably coincides with the watershed line of the Congo and Zambezi. On the

---

* Lewanika's sovereignty is acknowledged by twenty-five tribes. *Trans.*

east it is bounded by the River Kafukwe, and on the west by the line of 20° east longitude from Greenwich. The southern frontier is in part the natural one of the Zambezi and Linyanti rivers.

Borotsiland is, consequently, approximately enclosed between 12° and 18° south latitude and 20° and 29° east longitude.

Prerogatives of the King. The king, an absolute autocrat, has the right of life and death over all his subjects. The inhabitants, the soil, and all within it or upon it, the products of the earth and the fish of the rivers and the wild beasts all belong in theory to the king.

Government. All important questions concerning the safety of the state and the government of his subjects are submitted to him. He frequently administers justice in the morning and afternoon in *lekhothla*, the "deliberative assembly." His judgments have the quality of law, and he in himself represents the Courts of Justice, Appeal, and Cassation. In ordinary cases the decision of the chiefs is put before him. Every man may be present at the *lekhothla*.

Administration. The kingdom of the Barotsi is divided into what in France are called *arrondissements*. The more important chiefs are chosen by the king, and are for the most part Barotsi.

These chiefs must live in the capital and take part in the *lekhothla* under the king.

In this country polygamy has a political importance; in fact each one of the king's wives represents a tribe or a group of villages.

The subaltern chiefs, who are also appointed by the king, reside in the villages, where they receive the orders of their superior chiefs. They regulate every-day affairs, and see that the tribute is regularly sent to the king.

Oligarchic Laws. The amount of the property of each chief is regulated according to his rank. No one may build huts as large or wear ornaments as costly as those of his superior in dignity.

In particular, the skins of lions, leopards, wild cats, and otters revert directly to the king, who distributes them in accordance with the oligarchic rules of the country.

Pins and bracelets of ivory, certain shapes of domestic utensils, a certain cut of hair, and the custom of blackening the teeth with lime are reserved exclusively for the royal family.

It is the same for all the categories of chiefs. It is needless to add that the latter live in general by extortion and pillage.

Slaves. Villages and groups of huts are known by the names of their chiefs. The chiefs can carry off a child from a family whose members are not Barotsi; the child then becomes a slave. All his labour he gives to his master, who has the right of life and death over him, and he can be liberated only by the king himself. The king and his elder sister, Queen Mokwai, receive every year as tribute a number of children of both sexes, who become their servants. According to their good pleasure, they give those of their servants they have no need of to their chiefs or other persons.

A Morotsi can never become a slave.

Slave-raids. In time of war large slave raids are undertaken. The slaves must be presented to the king before they can become the property of their masters.

Forced Labour. All the king's subjects, excepting the Barotsi, are liable to enforced labour. Lewanika's fields, which cover the country, are cultivated by forced labourers. These labourers are usually women, who till the ground and build huts.

From top to bottom of the social scale the chiefs have the power of levying labour, and the unhappy labourer, who often belongs to several masters, must at the first requisition abandon his or her personal work, and can claim neither food nor payment.

Forced labourers also undertake the work of messengers, boatmen, fishermen, porters, wood-cutters, reapers of grass and rushes, &c., &c.

APPENDIX I

In addition, certain tribes must annually send the king a fixed impost of canoes, building wood, cattle, grain, milk, wild honey, fish, game, skins, iron spear-heads, mattocks, &c. Here is a singular custom: When the imposts are taken to the king he selects over-night what he himself requires; they are then carried into the public place, where the king makes a second choice of a portion of them; the remainder he then distributes among his chiefs.   *Tributes and Imposts.*

Ivory is one of the chief sources of Lewanika's revenue. One may reckon that at Lealuyi the pound of ivory is worth five to six shillings.

Mabutu, usually the sons of chiefs, are the young men composing the king's bodyguard. They are aged from fifteen to thirty years; they sleep before the king's door, or in the immediate neighbourhood of his residence. Each has his special task; some are detailed to prepare the king's food, to cut his wood and grind his corn, while others prepare his skins and his bedding. They must follow with the king in all his movements.   *Mabutu.*

The *Mabutu* may become chiefs of greater or less importance, or men of affairs, and according to their capacity can arrive at the dignity of *Likombwa*. The latter are men of all ages, whom the king himself chooses: they are his personal servants. They have huts set apart for them; they superintend the various services of the king's house, overlook the slaves, lay up the grain in the granaries, inspect the cattle, &c. Their position is much envied. In political matters the *Likombwa* must always take the part of the king, and in *lekhothla* they sit at his left hand.   *The Likombwa.*

The most conspicuous office in the country is that of the *Gambela*, or Prime Minister, who makes himself cognisant of all affairs and reports them to the king in their briefest form. Then come other ministers. The ministers of the royal family take part in the *lekhothla*.   *The Gambela, or Prime Minister.*

A curious anomaly among the Barotsi has already been   *Mokwai.*

mentioned. As in all countries not under the influence of Christianity, woman is very far from being the equal of man, and yet here the king's elder sister enjoys the same rights as her brother, and receives the same tribute. She carries the title of Mokwai, signifying Queen, and has her own residence.

Punishments and Penalties.

The list of punishments and penalties would take much space to enumerate. For a mere nothing, a delay, an order ill executed, or an utensil broken, the servant, slave, or child will have his throat squeezed by his master's hands until he falls to the ground unconscious. Sometimes the victim does not come to life again, as recently happened at Sesheke,

Garotting.

where a servant, who made use of an object she should not have touched, was punished by the princess's order in this manner. And what shall be said of the terrible whip whose every blow bespatters the flesh with blood!

Last year, at Kazungula, a little girl stole some maize. The owner of the field, an old woman, seized the child and held her hand in the fire until it was charred through and through. The child died the next day.

A goat-stealer was punished in another way: the unhappy man was bound hand and foot and laid on his back for a whole day with his face to the scorching sun. At the close of the day the chief, not considering this punishment sufficient, cut off his ears with his own hands.

A malefactor will be bound, placed in the path of a band of *seruyi*, the terrible warrior ants, and be gradually devoured alive by them. At Lealuyi, however, M. Coillard has succeeded in suppressing the terrible ordeal by water; the unfortunate creature who was accused of casting a spell on one of his fellows was forced to plunge his hands into boiling water. Once the hands were blistered the accused was placed forcibly on a rack and a violent poison given him; he was then burned while still living.

Religion.

As for the religion of the Zambezians, I cannot do better than quote, with his permission, M. Coillard's description of it:—

"Among the Zambezians the religious sentiment is more

developed than among any other tribe in this part of Africa. Without making use of idols and fetishes, they worship not only the shades of their ancestors, whom they consult or placate at need with a sacrifice, but also a supreme being (Nyambe) who is symbolised by the Sun, the Moon symbolising his wife. This woman became the mistress of their deity in the legendary Night. She gave birth to the animals, then to Man. Presently there was a conflict between Nyambe and Man. Nyambe manifested his power in resuscitating the animals Man killed, but on the other hand Man was so cunning that Nyambe became afraid, and mounted to heaven by a spider's web, since when, they say, he has been invisible. The people of certain tribes believe in metempsychosis, and every man during his lifetime chooses the animal whose body he wishes to enter. He then performs an initiatory rite, which consists of swallowing the maggots bred in the putrid carcase of the animal of his choice; he thenceforth partakes of its nature. And on the occasion of a calamity, while the women are giving themselves up to lamentations, you will see one man writhing on the ground like a boa or a crocodile, another howling and leaping like a panther, a third baying like a jackal, roaring like a lion, or grunting like a hippopotamus, imitating the character of the various animals to perfection."

Superstitions and Sorcerers.
The Barotsi are very superstitious, and carry amulets consisting of pieces of wood, horn, bark, or grain, either to keep their enemies at a distance, or from other motives. They believe that they are not such good shots as the white man because the latter carries a charm in the hand with which they are unacquainted.

They place " medicines "* in the spoor of dangerous animals to prevent their approach. Before fording a river with their herds they throw " medicine " on the water to drive away the crocodiles. They have charms of many kinds, including one to drive away locusts.

The sorcerers or witch-doctors go from village to village with remedies which they cook in great cauldrons to make rain.

* Charms or fetishes. *Trans.*

They believe the dead come back in the form of snakes, hyenas, crocodiles, &c., to torment the living.

Before setting out for the chase or war, a chief will go to the grave of his father, place on it his spear and a bucket of water, and intercede with his shade.

Cattle are led past graves to obtain conception.

The Family: Polygamy. Family ties, outside the influence of Christianity, are extremely relaxed. Polygamy is practised: the women whose position is greatly inferior to that of the men, have to work in the fields and feed their husband; they wait on him, and never eat with him. Marriages are easily made and unmade, which causes much immorality.

Birth. Except in the case of a royal child, a birth is not considered a fortunate event. Civil rights do not exist in any shape, only the missionaries having introduced them in their stations. Children are left to themselves; they have to look after themselves when very young. Among the Barotsi the old are respected and consulted, which is not always the case with the other subject peoples.

Death. When a chief is about to die he is immediately wrapped in a blanket, and buried a few hours after his death. If he dies in the daytime he is buried at sunset; if he dies at night he is buried before the dawn. They do not always wait for the death of a dying man before digging his grave, and he is often buried with the death-rattle in his throat. His wives remove all their ornaments and amulets, and mourn for the dead man for three days and nights, after which the chief's huts are demolished, and the heads of his widows shaven. These women then become the property of the chief who replaces the dead man.

Burial. The Barotsi, in general, have no cemeteries, and a man may bury his dead where he chooses. A chief considers it an honour to be buried in the middle of his kraal, that is to say in his cattle-pen. The grave of a father is respected, and his offspring visit it on great occasions.

The royal graves are surrounded by a hedge of green trees; they are regarded throughout the country as oracles, and are invoked in times of calamity, pestilence, or drought. Cattle and grain are offered up there. In time of war arms are taken thither to be blessed.

The type varies to infinity among the different tribes, and there is a great mixture of blood among them. **Characteristics.**

The sovereign race of the Barotsi consists chiefly of tall and well-made men; the forehead is often full, the eyes intelligent, the oval of the face regular, and the beard scanty; the lips are not very thick.

The women frequently rub their bodies with fat, which gives them a clear bronzed colour.

Along the shores of the Zambezi we saw some men of superb muscular development. On the banks of the Njoko we met Matotela who, save for their complexions, had some resemblance to the Jew.

In their natural state the Barotsi are frivolous and immoral, generous from self-interest, ironical and mocking. Taking no precautions in times of abundance, they can content themselves with very little in a time of want. They are very skilful workers in iron and wood; in a word, they are industrious, intelligent, and observant. They are excellent paddlers and good walkers.

The Serotsi, one of the numerous Bantu dialects, is the official language. It is unwritten. The Barotsi are polyglot, and nearly all understand Sekololo, a corruption of Sesuto. They freely make use of several idioms in modifying words, and numerous dialects are spoken by the various tribes. **Language and Literature.**

Their literature consists of tales and songs, which are transmitted orally from father to son, and which concern themselves with noble feats in battle or in the chase.

They possess many musical instruments; amongst others the *scrimba*, which consists of a row of hollow calabashes with a tongue of sonorous wood fixed on each; the tongues are struck with a little hammer. They have various kinds of **Music.**

drums; and also the *kangombio*, in which ten tongues of metal are fixed round a plate of hardwood, which in turn is fixed on an empty calabash. These ten tongues give a minor octave. The Barotsi carry this latter instrument with them on their journeys; often in our camp at night one of our porters would sing the incidents of the day, accompanying himself on the *kangombio*, which produced a sort of dirge, melancholy, and sometimes very sweet.

Art. Art, with the Zambezians, is still in its first period. However, they work pleasing decorations on their wood and metal, and carve in ivory. With the roots of a certain tree they weave baskets whose quality, form, and design denote the possession of an already pronounced artistic sense.

Industry. From the industrial point of view the Zambezians are very skilful workers in iron and wood. Thanks to the iron found in the country, in an almost pure state, which they work in high furnaces of their own invention, they succeed in obtaining a durable metal. Although their tools, &c., are more than rudimentary, they make excellent arms — spears, axes, and knives.

The Barotsi have also a special aptitude for all mechanical work, and M. Coillard wishes to develop the natives in this direction by founding an industrial school.

From the skin of a plant which grows during the flood season, and is gathered when the waters retire, they make cords and thread which rival our European products.

The women work in pottery, which they fire; the men prepare furs and skins admirably, of which they make magnificent mantles for their chiefs.

Commerce. Commerce with the exterior is almost nil; Portuguese half-breeds pay periodical visits to Borotsiland to buy ivory and slaves, but Lewanika, thanks to the influence of the Zambezi missionaries, is gradually opposing himself to traffic in the latter.

Agriculture. The natives cultivate principally the following products of the soil: sorghum, mealies, millet, earth-nuts, sweet potatoes, manioc, gourds, water-melons, and tobacco.[*]

They breed cattle of two species: one, the Borotsi breed, is large; and the other, originally from the Moshukulumbwe country, is smaller. They have also sheep and goats of the degenerate Botoka breeds, and also skinny poultry.

They are extremely partial to the honey of the wild bee, *mouka*, as well as that of the little honey-fly, *ntsi*.

They do no serious work as shepherds or breeders; the cows give so little milk that often they can scarcely nourish their own calves.

The inhabitants believe fresh milk to be unwholesome, and use only curdled milk. Some of them find that the best method of curdling milk is never to clean the vessels employed to hold it.

The natural resources of the country are not yet known. But in addition to the iron ore one must mention the great forests of many kinds of trees; amongst the principal ones we may notice:— **Natural Resources. Forests.**

The *mochengi*, with a lofty trunk, evergreen leaves, and very hard wood. The *motsaoli* or *massiri*, a tree of majestic size and form, recalling the oak; its wood resembles that of the mahogany, and is used by the natives in preference to others in the construction of their canoes. Once sawn, the great trunks can be used as building timber. This tree bears a red berry to which the natives are very partial. The *mochabu* is also a very lofty tree, sometimes reaching an enormous height; it grows in moist places; the wood is soft and the bark purgative.

The *mohonoro*, used in building, is very hard and durable. The *mobula*, which resembles the maple or hornbeam, is used for cabinet-work, and bears an edible stone-fruit. The *motondo*, a tree with light foliage and straight grain, is used for making the handles of axes and mattocks. The *mokau* is less beautiful than the preceding; with its wood are made paddles, small unsinkable canoes, and household utensils; it bears no fruit.

[*] Called in the language of the country: *mabili, mpongi, maoutsa, masambani, sembukuma, mangia, maputsi, lehapua, kuci*. *Author*.

Then there is the *majongolo*, which is used for making ladles, and bears edible fruit. We may once more notice the *moholuholu*, a shrub; its fruit, which externally resembles a great orange, may cause dysentery in a European.

Rubber.   The caoutchouc tree grows spontaneously.

Cotton.   The natives weave a coarse stuff from the pods of the wild cotton. We noticed orchids, but unhappily it was not their blossoming season.

Animals.   The wild animals are numerous and varied, according to the district: buffalo, lions, leopards or panthers, hyenas, jackals. The elephants and rhinoceroses, of which we have seen the traces, but which we have never got near, are apparently becoming less frequent.

There is a great variety of antelopes, from the little *oribi* (*Nanotragus scoparius*), one of the smallest antelopes known, the steinbuck (*Nanotragus tragulus*), and the duiker (*Cephalophus mergens*), up to the massive eland (*Oreas canna*), which may weigh 800 lbs. to 1,000 lbs. The koodoo (*Strepsiceros kudu*), with spiral horns; the sable antelope (*Hippotragus niger*), with high withers; the graceful waterbuck (*Cobus ellipsiprymnus*), with a dappled coat; the reedbuck (*Cervicapra arundinacea*), with reddish hair; the *lechwe* (*Cobus leche*), a dweller in marshes; the *babale*, or Lichtenstein's Hartebeest (*Alcephalus lichtensteini*), with elongated head and inverted horns, &c.

Let us notice further among the antelopes:—
The borer antelope (*Hippotragus leucopheus*).
The *pookoo* (*Cobus vardoni*).
The bush-buck (*Tragelaphus sylvaticus*).
The king-buck (*Epyceros melampus*).
The *situtunga* (*Tragelaphus spekii*).
The *tsessebe* (*Alcephalus lunatus*).
The warthog (*Phacochoerus aethiopicus*) lives also in these regions.

We have on various occasions met with herds of the blue gnu (*Catoblepus gorgon*) and the zebra (Burchell's zebra), counting many hundred head. The ostrich and giraffe, which are found to the south of the Zambezi, do not exist in the parts of Borotsiland to the north of the great river.

Numerous hippopotami and crocodiles inhabit the waters of the Zambezi; we saw them also in the Machili. I must also mention the snakes of all lengths.*

The Borotsi possesses numbers of aquatic birds: the ibis, heron, pelican, crane, and plover; various species of geese, ducks, and teal. There is also the white fishing-eagle with black wings, three or four species of francolin (a genus between pheasant and partridge), two species of guinea-fowl, &c. *Birds.*

There are mice, rats, and other rodents, which seek refuge in the huts at the time of the floods. *Rodents.*

The insects are numbered by legions, and are a perfect plague: such as the *sernyi*, or warrior ants, whose close-packed hordes turn aside for nothing; the termites, wrongly called white ants, are especially mischievous, and attack everything excepting greasy substances. The *kokoani-nisu*, small black ants, get into one's food, provisions, &c. The locusts, *tsie*, have red bodies and wings barred with white and black; they completely devour the crops in a very short time. Flies and mosquitoes, little and big, torment the traveller. *Insects.*

The *sebuhi* are venomous spiders; the *sekokes* are enormous but inoffensive flat spiders that run along the walls of the huts. The scorpions are all more or less venomous. *Spiders.*

I will end the list by the *tsetse*. This fly frequents certain well-defined regions. Its bite is not followed by fatal consequences in the case of man or the wild animals, but it is fatal, *The Tsetse Fly.*

* Not far from the banks of the Machili our men killed a snake of a deep greyish brown, whose structure astonished us. It was nearly eight feet long, and the thickest part of its body measured 5¾ in. in circumference. The head was very small and slightly flattened. The last twenty inches of its length are much slighter than the rest, and the end of the tail is scarcely larger than a knitting-needle. It seems that this snake is venomous. *Author.*

sooner or later, to almost all the domestic animals, above all to cattle, oxen, horses, and dogs ; the ass resists it longest.

We observed that the tsetse frequents the same regions as the buffalo. Is it perhaps one of the parasites of the buffalo, and does it acquire its venom from the excrement of that animal or elsewhere? The scientist who shall succeed in determining the virus of this insect and in inoculating the domestic animals of Africa against it, as has been done in Europe against anthrax and other cattle diseases, would render a signal service, for vast stretches of country are made inaccessible by the presence of this terrible tsetse, which is scarcely larger than a house-fly.

The domestic animals immune to the venom of the tsetse form a very small minority. They are called "salted," and are highly prized.

New Species.

Since his return to Europe M. Louis Jalla, the missionary, has presented to the museum of zoology and comparative anatomy of the University of Turin a zoological collection made during his ten years' residence in Upper Zambezia. This collection includes specimens of Ophidieus, Lacertians, Orthoptera, Diplopodes, and Arachnides.[*]

He has thereby added many new species to those already known ; some of them have justly been named after him.

I may mention among others, in the class of Arachnides, the new species *Hyllus Jalla*, and in the Diplopodes the new species *Odontopyge Jalla*, *Odontopyge exquisita*, *Archipirostreptus Jalla*, *Archipirostreptus dexter*, *Lophostreptus Camerauni*.

Reckoning of Time.

As for the reckoning of time, the Barotsi have the lunar year ; every one knows the different phases. At each new moon there is an interruption of work, and dances are held during the afternoon and evening.

Thanks to the influence of the missionaries, King Lewanika himself observes the Christian Sunday to-day.

The natives have very vague notions as to their ages ; they

[*] See the Journal of the Museum in question for 1896, vol. ix., parts 255, 257, 271, 209.

will say, for example, "I was born at the time of such a war, such a famine, such a flood."

Seasons. The year ends for the Barotsi at the time of harvest, but on no determined day.

The year has two divisions: *Letchlabala*, or summer, and *Mariha*, or winter.

The summer is further divided into *mouabi*, from August 15th to the end of November. The hottest period of the year is from the end of October to mid-November, a time when the winds blow and the heat is intense. This is the dry season, preceding the rainy season, or *Letchlabula*, properly so called, which lasts from November to the end of February. From mid-February to the month of May is the period of inundations, or *munda*.

Mariha, or the true winter, begins at the end of May and ends in mid-August.

It is needless to say that these dates are not fixed, and that they vary according to the years.

Temperature. "A few observations of temperature made during ten years by M. Louis Jalla, at Kazungula.

HOT SEASON.

Maximum (Fahrenheit).

116·6°* in the shade from 2.0 to 4.0 p.m. | End of
68° to 71·6° by night. | October.

Mean

102° to 104° by day, | End of October.
68° to 71·6° by night. |

COLD SEASON.

Mean.

75° to 77° by day, | May, June, and July.
43° to 50° by night. |

These are all shade temperatures.

* This temperature, once recorded, is not perhaps the annual maximum.

In the course of the hot season the thermometer, being placed in the sun,* rose to 110°, and had to be removed to prevent bursting."

In the interior of the country, on the high uplands, the differences of temperature are very great.

Reid and I saw a heavy white frost on the night of July 31st, when camping near the source of the Machili.

I may give in this connection the following observations which I made while crossing, in a north-westerly direction, that part of Borotsiland lying between Lealuyi and the Machili.

In camp, on August 7th, on the right bank of the Kwemba river, the temperature at 6.30 a.m. was 36·5°.

On August 9, in camp on the banks of the Lumbi, the temperature in the sun before my tent, at 3.0 p.m., was 107·6°. At 6.0 a.m. the next morning, in the same place, it was only 33·8°.

On August 12, at 6.0 a.m., a few hours march from the Motondo (an affluent of the Lui), the thermometer descended to freezing point.

Rainfall.   M. Coillard has registered the annual rainfall of Upper Zambezia for several years. He gives a mean of 33·7 inches. This mean is constant. If the quantity of rain that has fallen up to the time of the rainy season (*Letchlabula*) is below the average, there are invariably great storms at the end of the season, which bring the rainfall up to the figure given.

Climate.   The climate is, on the whole, unhealthy. The natives suffer principally from fever and small-pox. The latter malady is followed by various affections of the eye. The missionaries have introduced vaccine into the country, and have vaccinated hundreds of natives.

* The temperature of a body in the sun depends largely upon the ratio between its absorbing and radiating powers, and is no test whatever of the temperature of the air. *Trans.*

The most dangerous period is that following the flood season, as the retiring waters leave on the earth a detritus that decomposes under the rays of the burning sun.

I should like, further, to quote the following remarks, which I recently heard M. Coillard make at a lecture which he had been invited to give before a geographical society.

Reflections by M. Coillard.

Is it necessary to insist on the weight given to the following lines by the thirty-five or forty years that this heroic man has devoted to Africa?

"I have said nothing of the abyss of corruption in which these populations lie, nor of the moral and physical sufferings of which they are the victims; the subject is too lamentable and too vast.

"From afar, no doubt, these primitive peoples, heedless, improvident, never sure of the morrow—these people who sing in the moonlight—may appear from Europe surrounded by a certain halo of poetry. And yet, I say, they have never known what it is to be happy.

"Listen to their songs in the minor key—they are lamentations. Hear them tell you that their hearts are black—that is to say sad—black, yes, black as their skins, and thus from the cradle to the grave do they carry always through life the symbol and livery of their suffering. Gentlemen, why do we occupy ourselves with geography? It is because the world is our native land; because, be their race, their colour, their nationality, or their rank what it may, all men are our brothers.

"For centuries Africa has been for Europe, no less than for herself, the mysterious continent, dark and unknown. To-day she is revealing herself to the world, and compelling its attention. She is being transformed with a rapidity that startles us.

"After having for centuries snatched away her children to throw them on the markets, there to sell them like beasts of burden, Europe to-day is tearing out the riches of her entrails. And allured by the bait of riches yet unknown, behold our European emigration, which rises and throws its foam towards the very heart of the continent, like a mighty tide that no dyke can wrest. And amid this strange commotion what will the Africans themselves become? Where will the negro race go to? What will be their future? Will it be that of the North American Indian? God forbid! The heart of a man and a Christian revolts at the mere suggestion of such an outlook. One thing that reassures us is the astonishing vitality of the race. Sixty odd years ago, for example, what was the Basuto nation? A few scattered hamlets among the mountains about Moshili, which the missionaries surrounded with solicitude like the solicitude of a mother for her sick child. About 1870 the Government took a first census, which gave 60,000 inhabitants. "And the last census shows that there are exactly 260,000 inhabitants, without counting the thousands dispersed throughout Cape Colony.

"What will the Basutos become in twenty, thirty, or forty years, if nothing arises to destroy their independence?

"The same facts are seen everywhere. Therefore the negro race has a future. But what future? Without doubt, that which the moral, intellectual, and material might of the white race chooses to make it. But for the philanthropist, and the Christian philanthropist, there is a duty to accomplish, a task imposes itself, and one worthy of the greatest generosity, and the sacrifice of the rarest lives. It is the work of rescue."

APPENDIX II

Notes on the Papers read before the Royal Geographical Society, London, January 4, 1897, concerning an Exploring Expedition into Borotsiland, by Captain Alfred St. Hill Gibbons, Mr. Percy C. Reid, and Captain Alfred Bertrand.

It is unnecessary to repeat that the expedition was organised at Mafeking, some 800 miles from the Cape, then the terminus of the railroad.

The direction followed was northerly; through Molepolole, in the territory of the Bakwena tribe; through Kanye, where the Ba-ngwaketsi are quartered; and past the Kalahari desert to Palapye, the residence of Khama, king of the Bamangwato. The expedition then skirted the eastern shores of Makarikari, the great salt lake, finally traversing the country called "The Land of the Thousand Vleys."

In short, the expedition made the distance between Mafeking and the Zambezi—which it struck near its confluence with the Linyanti—in sixty-four days.

After crossing to the left bank of the Zambezi and entering the kingdom of the Barotsi the expedition properly so called began.

At this point Captain Gibbons left his companions in order to go straight up the Zambezi, as far as Lealuyi, and thence to explore the country in various directions.

Here, in a few lines, is a brief *résumé* of this remarkable exploration as told in the paper read before the Royal Geographical Society:—

While going up the Zambezi to Lealuyi, the residence of

King Lewanika, Captain Gibbons made a large number of astronomical and solar observations, by this means rectifying at several points the course of the river as traced on the maps.

From Lealuyi he began to explore the country in an easterly direction. On the edge of the Borotsi Plain he discovered the basin of a lake which receives the waters of the Kande river.

In three days he reached the Lui river, sixty-three miles from Lealuyi, in 15° 28′ S. lat. Passing along the southern bank of the Maüngu he crossed the sources of the Luwowa and Koshamba, which flow into the Motondo, the most important of the Lui tributaries, the sources of which he reached on October 7th, in 15° 27′ 17″ S. lat. and 24° 39′ E. long. approximately. "The Motondo rises on high ground, with much open country, at a height of 3,980 feet, or 580 feet above the Borotsi Plain, from which it is about eighty-two miles as the crow flies."

Continuing his easterly course, Captain Gibbons came to the source of the Lumbi, which he placed in 15° 28′ 1″ S. lat., and then found a small stream called the Nyambe Noka, a tributary to the Luompa on the left bank. The Luompa flows into the Luena, which, according to Lewanika, flows into a large lake to the south of the confluence of the Kapombo and the Zambezi.

"Further information showed me that the Luazanza, rising about 15° 20′ S. lat. and 25° 30′ E. long., also flows into the Luompa, left bank ; so that the Luompa must rise farther north, and the Luena probably still farther to the north-west, its system completing the blank space in the maps bounded by the Kapombo, Kafukwe, Lui, and Lumbi watersheds, and draining this extensive area in an almost westerly direction.

"Following the Nyambe to its source, 15° 43′ 7″ S. lat. and 3,860 feet (a drop of sixty feet from the Lumbi) above the sea-evel, I travelled south for some twenty miles to what the natives call the source of the Njoko river, crossing the Kashi, one of the largest of the Lumbi tributaries, on the way. . . . I now decided to follow the course of the Njoko to my former camp at its confluence with the Rampungu."

From Rampungu Captain Gibbons reached the Luanga, and regained his point of departure at Kazungula at the junction of the Zambezi with the Linyanti, Chobe, or Kwando. He was

APPENDIX II

there attacked by dysentery, which reduced him almost to a skeleton.

Once afoot again, Captain Gibbons undertook another exploration to the north-east into Boshikolumbwe, or the land of the Mashikolumbwe, a people much dreaded by other tribes.

He gained the watershed of the tributaries to the Sejlefula on the left bank, crossed three or four tributaries to the left bank of the Machili, and entered the basin of the Kafukwe. Crossing the Nanzela, he came to the Nkala.

Continuing his course along the basin of the Kafukwe, which he crossed at Kaigu, he then took a north-easterly course to Kowetu, his farthest point; altitude, 4,000 feet. At Musanana he discovered hot calcareous springs.

Finally he returned to Kazungula, his point of departure, after numerous adventures; in particular, he rid the neighbourhood of Nkala of a lion, which, according to the inhabitants, had eaten during the last thirteen days of his life two women, two oxen, two donkeys, a sheep, a goat, and a lamb.

Captain Gibbons made *en route* a number of solar and astronomical observations to determine the positions of many important points; he also collected much information concerning Boshikolumbweland.

Captain Gibbons's travels in the kingdom of the Barotsi covered a distance of more than 1,800 miles.

While he was returning from the Zambezi he was for three days—quite unawares—in imminent danger of falling into the hands of the Matabele, who were then in full revolt. But for this providential chance he would have been one of their numerous victims.

After parting with Captain Gibbons, Mr. Percy Reid, Mr. Pirie, and myself proceeded to ascend the Machili, a tributary to the Zambezi, on the left bank.

Mr. Reid had also approximately to plot out the course of the river and to determine the source. He made a certain number of solar and astronomical observations to fix the position of important points, and I often had occasion to assist him by reading the chronometer while he handled the sextant.

I cannot do better than reproduce the principal passages of the paper which Mr. Reid read before the Royal Geographical Society:—

"The Machili rises on the southern slope of a high sand-ridge, at an altitude of about 3,900 feet above sea-level. There is no absolute source, such as a bubbling spring, but merely a slight ill-defined valley about 100 yards wide, carpeted with grass and edged on both sides with forest. As one follows down the valley, it is joined by other small valleys similar, but smaller, and chiefly on the east bank, and at the junction of these with the main bed the ground becomes wet and oozy. The descent is fairly rapid, say fifty feet in a couple of miles, and then comes a slight outcrop of stones, and the first real water is found in a few rocky pools in the river's bed. The course is north-east to south-west, and in a few miles the sides of the valley have become steeper and the river full of water, in which a current is plainly visible. Some five miles down a considerable stream joins the Machili from the east, and a large pool is formed at the juncture, and below this the river is flowing strongly. Following the same general direction lat. 16° 21′ is reached, and there, after emerging from stony ground, the valley opens out to a width of some 150 yards, and the river itself gradually dries up, and is soon quite lost, except for one or two stagnant pools in its bed. Some few miles lower the country on either side becomes again stony, and the river at once reappears, and, gaining volume, is soon running rapidly and noisily forward, in many places like a Scotch burn. About lat. 16° 35′ it makes a sudden and sharp bend to the east, and, after flowing some six or eight miles in this direction, emerges from the stony hills on to a wide 'turf' valley (with an altitude of about 3,400 feet), where it again suddenly bends to the south and becomes apparently stagnant, and in places almost dry. Another and similar but smaller bend to the east and then south occurs in lat. 16° 48′, the valley again contracting and a certain flow of water becoming perceptible. From this point onwards for some forty-five miles the same characteristics prevail, and then again the river becomes a series of deep pools with dry spaces in between. Here the river has become sufficiently large for the pools to contain hippopotami. The country now has become flatter, the valley of the river has disappeared, and the river continues in alternate pools and dry spaces until some five or six miles before the Kasaia is reached, when the pools of water cease entirely, and the river-bed itself also vanishes utterly. Of course, I am speaking now of the dry season. In the rains the river is full of water and flowing throughout; but the curious fact remains that when I saw it, it was alternately flowing and stagnant, and that even in the wet season it empties itself into a large marsh, which in its turn drains rather than flows into the Kasaia. Wherever the subsoil is rocky and the fall somewhat pronounced, there we find water running throughout the year: where the country becomes more level and the soil alluvial turf (it is nowhere sandy), there the river is represented by pools, or loses itself entirely.

"Viewing the river from its mouth upwards, the rise is very slight until you reach lat. 16° 35′, when you first get really out of the Zambezi valley and into stony hills. Rising through these, you find beyond them a main high sandy ridge, which forms the watershed between the Kafukwe river and the Zambezi. This ridge runs approximately north-west to south-east, and is the origin of all the rivers flowing into the left bank of the Zambezi between Kazungula and the capital Lialui.

"Vegetation throughout the country traversed is thick. In the alluvial parts it consists of high forest trees without much undergrowth; in the more stony and barren parts the forest is smaller and the undergrowth thicker—in places almost impenetrable jungle. Temperature in the winter months is very pleasant—about 80° to 85° in the shade at midday, and with cool refreshing nights. We experienced a sharp frost on July 31 at the source of the river, in lat. 16° 9′. Population is sparse, but it is hard to judge population in Africa, as the villages are hidden away in the bush, and the natives rarely show themselves. Several tribes that go to form the Barotsi nation inhabit the district. They cultivate several sorts of cereals and pulses, as well as tobacco, pumpkins, and several sorts of roots. They are clothed, if at all, in skins, and use skins to cover themselves at night. They are all armed with assegais, a very few have guns, still fewer have ammunition, and one tribe, the Mankoyas, all carry bows and poisoned arrows. They are nearly all adepts at trapping game, either in pitfalls or snares. They are quite peaceably disposed, shy by nature, but soon become used to the presence of white men. They are indifferent carriers, and desert on slight provocation; but they rarely steal their loads, although they abandon them by the road. They are destitute of pluck, and would be of no use in a time of danger.

"The game of the country is, or was, very numerous. I say 'was,' because I am sorry to hear that the rinderpest has devastated Borotsiland as it has Matabeleland and Mashonaland, and that the game now is practically extinct, the carcases lying rotting in all directions. Elephant are very scarce—I did not see one; rhinoceros scarcer still; hippopotami are found in the Zambezi and Machili; while all over the country were buffalo, Burchell's zebra, many sorts of antelope, and many lions. Neither giraffe nor ostrich are found east of the Zambezi."

The following is an outline of my own paper, read at the same meeting, and subsequently revised and amplified:—

After having explored the course of the Machili, Mr. Reid considered that his task was in part completed; we accordingly agreed to meet later at Kazungula, at the confluence of the Linyanti with the Zambezi, and I decided to cross Borotsiland, in a north-westerly direction, as far as Lealuyi, the residence of King Lewanika.

August 1st.—I set out with twenty-four men and encamped at nightfall on the banks of the Kakoma, a tributary to the Machili on the right bank.

August 2nd.—After crossing the marshy bed of the Wannaroba, another tributary of the Machili—a quaking, grass-covered bog, through which we floundered up to our knees in mire—and that of the Kamitwe, which was also at that time a swamp, we came to the Kamanga, flowing probably into the Njoko, which lies to the south-west. We were then in the basin of the Njoko, and encamped not far from the Mania, a tributary on the left bank.

During these two days we crossed a series of crooked ridges very close to one another and separated by little valleys.

We saw no natives, nor any traces of huts. Big game was rare; it would seem to emigrate to other districts at this season of the year, for we found abundance of it while ascending the Machili.

August 3rd.—Clusters of huts or villages, which, according to custom, bore the name of their chief, Meori. We were on the frontier of the Mankoya country, which we were leaving for that of the Matotela, a tribe very superior to the former. The Mankoya are solely hunters, while the Matotela are also agriculturists and workers in iron.

The Matotela, whose costume is the simplest possible, are armed with assegais; some of them carry, in addition to this, a light tapering spear for taking fish. They commonly extract the two upper central incisor teeth. It is worthy of notice that many of them have a regular profile recalling the Jewish type.

Near the confluence of the Mania and Njoko we found the village of the chief, Sihoupa. An enclosure of large boughs from six to ten feet high contains a large central hut surrounded by eleven smaller ones, round, built of reeds, and covered with thatch. There are fine trees in this neighbourhood, in particular the *motsaoli* or *massici*. The foliage of the *motsaoli* is dark green, and it bears a red fruit like a flattened bean, much relished by the natives.

The valley of the Njoko presents a pleasing appearance, bounded as it is by wooded hills, on the slopes of which brown patches are to be seen here and there, representing villages surrounded by their plantations of sorghum, ground-nuts, &c. I succeeded in obtaining a stock of these provisions in exchange for beads, blue glass ones are most in demand. There are cattle here.

August 5th.—We crossed over to the right bank of the Njoko, the water scarcely reaching to our knees. During the rainy season it is navigable as far as the Zambezi. On the side of one of the hills found the residence of the chief, Surukurukuru. Before crossing the Kambona, a tributary of the Njoko, we passed through a forest of tall trees.

August 6th.—I discovered a small lake, about 500 yards long, surrounded with verdure, in a charming valley. I named it "Blue Water," on account of its lovely colour. From this lake the Ikwe derives its source. This river, as well as the Kuemba, which we presently crossed, the water reaching our shoulders, is a tributary to the Njoko on the right bank. The ground was boggy and quaking.

August 7th.—At 6.30 a.m. the thermometer registered 36·7° Fahr.

We left the basin of the Njoko for that of the Lumbi. During these two days we saw no traces of human beings.

August 8th.—We halted at the village of the chief Naiumba, below the junction of the Masetti and Lumbi. Here we laid in a stock of provisions, obtaining sorghum, beans, and curdled milk in exchange for white glass beads. Before reaching the main channel of the Lumbi, in order to cross over to its right bank, we floundered about in the sticky mud of its swampy margin. The Lumbi flows through a valley wider but less lovely than that of the Njoko. I saw some lechwe antelopes (*Cobus leche*) in these parts.

From the source of the Machili to the Lumbi our course lay across a succession of wooded ridges in close proximity to one another and separated by dingle and valleys.

The principal trees found in the forest and scrub, besides the *motsaoli*, a hardwood tree already mentioned, were the *mobula*, bearing an edible stone-fruit, the *motoudo*, with bright foliage, the *mokoa*, the *matjompolo*, &c. There were also numerous *moholuhola*, shrub-like trees bearing large round fruit with hard rinds.

August 10*th*.—I may mention in passing that although the days are often hot—for summer is approaching—the nights are sometimes cold.

This morning, in my camp on the banks of the Lumbi, the thermometer registered 31° Fahr. at 6 a.m., while yesterday afternoon, in the same place, and in the sun it indicated 108° Fahr.

Near the Lumbi we struck the track used by the missionaries when journeying by land from Kazungula to Lealuyi. We now crossed a wooded table-land, and near the little Musau lagoon we found the slots of elephants. We then passed the banks of the Kambai lagoon, which were succeeded by a wide plain covered with knots of trees. Here our feet sank in a warm white sand.

August 11*th*.—Wide plains with distant woods; we saw zebras and gnus at pasture. We skirted the Koara lake.

August 12*th*.—At 6.30 a.m. the thermometer went down to freezing point.

Wooded stretches were succeeded by stretches of sand, which we found very tiring to walk on. Then we came to a plain covered with ant-hills.

We crossed the Motondo, a tributary on the left bank to the Lui. The main channel, where the water was up to our middle, was bordered by a swamp of sticky mire.

August 13*th*.—After climbing a sandy wooded hill we had to cross yet another marsh before fording the Lui, on the right bank of which we found the village of the chief Moamanomni. Here I laid in a stock of sorghum, sweet potatoes, and curdled milk. This was in the country of the Makwenga, who possess cattle and are workers in iron.

More wooded hills.

August 14*th*.—Interminable sandy hills, more or less wooded ;

many green paraquets. After crossing a plain we came to the banks of the Nanjikua lake. Near at hand was the village of Shiribero, where we obtained manioc.

August 15*th*.—Hills more or less clad with trees alternating with plains. We came to the Mukango lake; between this and the Njoko lake is the village of Kulima, where I got manioc, dried potatoes, and milk both fresh and curdled, the former being a great rarity in this country. After passing the Njoko lake we found the country more and more thickly populated. We crossed, first, a tract of sand, then a wooded hillock, and so came to the place known as Katalba, to the west of which is a wide plain dotted with the huts of many large villages. Cattle was abundant. A plain covered with ant-hills, a swamp, and hills led us to the Ikulwe lake.

August 16*th*.—After climbing a long hill, where the silence was broken only by the cry of partridges, we entered the valley of Sefula, traversed by the river of that name, and bordered with many villages, of which the principal one, which is the site of a missionary station, also bears the name of Sefula.

August 17*th*.—We crossed a great plain enclosed by hills. This plain is undoubtedly the bed of an ancient lake. The villages are built on eminences raised by the termites. This plain is inundated during the rains. I arrived at Lealuyi, the residence of King Lewanika, and of the missionary, M. Coillard. My end was thus happily attained.

As one has seen, the country traversed may broadly be divided into two sections:—

(1) That portion of the Barotsi kingdom lying between the rivers Machili and Lumbi, which, according to King Lewanika, had not at that latitude been previously explored, and which is left blank on the maps. I have mentioned that this region is covered with a succession of wooded ridges, close together and separated by dales and valleys, through which flow the affluents of the three large tributaries to the Zambezi—the Machili, Njoko and Lumbi.

APPENDIX II

(2) Beyond the Lumbi we struck at various points the track used by the missionaries when going by land from Kazungula to Lealuyi. The nature of the country changes ; the ridges are further apart, the valleys wider, and the streams less numerous, the two most important being the Motondo and the Lui, which unite before joining the Zambezi.

There are many large lakes in these regions, some of which, it appears, communicate with the Zambezi, and receive the surplus waters during the rains.

The paper being read, several persons discussed it ; Sir John Kirk, who was Livingstone's companion in Africa in 1860 ; also Admiral Wharton, the vice-president in the chair, and several others.

In particular, I may note these words of Mr. Ravenstein, the distinguished cartographer of the Royal Geographical Society :

"Captain Gibbons's extensive journeys were checked by numerous observations for latitude ; Mr. Reid had substantially added to our knowledge by his survey of the Machili river ; whilst Captain Bertrand's journey from the head of that river to Lealuyi had connected the routes of his fellow-travellers, and filled up a vacant space upon the map."

Mr. Ravenstein contributes the following note to the "Proceedings":

"The map accompanying the above papers is to the greater extent based upon a survey by Captain Gibbons, checked by the latitudes of fifty-four places determined by meridian altitudes of the sun or of a star. These latitudes, which were re-computed by myself, inspire confidence. They not only are concordant, but also agree with the results of former travellers, and more especially those obtained by Dr. Livingstone. Thus, whilst Gibbons places Sesheke in lat. 17° 31' 18" S., Dr. Livingstone, whose observation was made on the southern bank of the river, obtained a latitude of 17° 31' 38" S. I do not understand the grounds on which Livingstone's latitude for that place has been rejected by certain map-makers.

"The longitude accepted for Lealuyi is dependent upon the observations made by Dr. Livingstone (at Naliele) and Serpa

Pinto (at Katongo), the meridian distance between these two places being assumed to amount to six minutes. Kazungula, below the confluence of the Zambezi with the Kuando, has retained the position assigned to this locality on my large map of Equatorial East Africa, published by the Society in 1881, viz., 25° 12' E.

"The Machili river has been inserted from a map furnished by Mr. Reid, checked by the determination of latitude of fourteen places. These latitudes were re-computed by Mr. Reeves and myself, and inspire every confidence.

"Captain Bertrand's route from the head of the Machili to Lealuyi is based upon a sketch-map supplied by that gentleman.

"All the altitudes inserted upon the map are from boiling-point observations made by Captain Gibbons and Mr. Reid. These have been computed by me to the best of my experience, but the results can only be looked upon as being approximate. The tribal name, Mambunda, inadvertently admitted by the lithographer, should be inserted between Lealuyi and Makwenga."*

We have all brought home specimens of the rich and varied fauna of Borotsiland.

Three lions fell to the bullets of Captain Gibbons; one of them, a man-eater, would appear to be the second in point of size of those killed in this part of Africa. The height at the shoulder was forty-three inches. The lion was set up, and shown at the meeting of the Royal Geographical Society, on January 4, 1897.

Captain Gibbons made also a collection of birds, and Mr. Reid a collection of butterflies.

During the course of the expedition I took a number of photographs of native types or landscape. Most of these were exhibited at the aforesaid meeting of the R.G.S. in London, and at the meeting of the Société de Géographie de Paris of January 22, 1897. I succeeded also in making an ethno-

---

* See the *Geographical Journal* (the organ of the Royal Geographical Society, London for February, 1897, vol. ix., No. 2.

graphical collection of various articles, illustrative of the arts and industries of the Barotsi. This was exhibited at the meeting of the eleventh Congress of the Swiss Geographical Societies held on May 26, 1896, in Geneva, under the auspices of the Geographical Society of that town, and also at the National Swiss Exposition, which was held in Geneva in 1896.

APPENDIX III

LEWANIKA was finally, though not securely, installed as King of the Barotsi in 1885. During one of the revolts that menaced his tenure of the throne he took refuge south of the Zambezi, and there became acquainted with the possibility and advantages of British protection. On his return to power he called an assembly of his vassal chiefs, in October, 1888, and proposed that they should place themselves under the protection of Queen Victoria. The proposal was not cordially received, and came near to costing him his newly regained power. He was advised by M. Coillard to take no further steps without consulting Khama.

In 1889 Mr. Ware obtained the Batoka mining concession. In June, 1890, the British South Africa Company obtained a treaty with Lewanika through their agent, Mr. Lochner. By this treaty the Company took over the Batoka concession, and obtained mining rights over the whole of Barotsi, from the Kafwe River to the line of 20 E. long., and from the Victoria Falls to the watershed of the Congo and Zambezi; these rights being held subject to a royalty of 4 per cent on the total output. The country was thrown open to traders, but was to be closed to immigrants. The Company engaged to defend the country from outside attack, and to send a representative with a staff of mounted police to Lealuyi, the capital. Owing to the unsettled state of Rhodesia, the first British resident—Major Coryndon—did not arrive until 1897.

The latest treaty was signed by an assembly of the chiefs at the Victoria Falls on June 25, 1898. By this treaty all administrative rights were conceded to the company, *excepting* the administration of native-cum-native affairs. Their mining rights were confirmed over the whole country, excepting only a district bounded by the Dongwe, Machili, Kabompo, and Zambezi rivers, but the natives retain the exclusive ownership of the iron mines already worked by them, as well as of certain timber-lands. The Company guarantees Lewanika's sovereignty over the twenty-five vassal tribes, undertakes to pay him an annuity in lieu of mining royalties, to protect his kingdom from outside aggression, and to protect him in the exercise of all the privileges and prerogatives of chieftainship that he has hitherto enjoyed ; that is to say, the Company administers only in respect of European or European-cum-native questions.

It undertakes also the matters of road, railway, and bridge-building, and the development of such vegetable and mineral resources as have not hitherto been worked or discovered— such as gold and diamond-mining, oil or coal working, coffee-planting, &c., should these prove profitable—while such natural wealth as the Barotsi have hitherto enjoyed the use of—such as iron, rubber, ivory (elephants and ivory belong to the king), fishing, hunting, forests, pasture, and arable land— are fully retained by them, with the exercise of all such industries as spring from these.

The Company further undertakes to aid civilisation by means of schools and industrial establishments, while Lewanika, whose chieftainship over the twenty-five vassal tribes is recognised and guaranteed, is responsible for their good behaviour, and undertakes to continue the efforts he has long been making to suppress slavery and witchcraft.

Pending the convention of an Anglo-Portuguese Boundary Commission the western and south-western boundaries of the Borotsi remain undefined, though the stream of the Zambezi forms, as a *modus vivendi*, the temporary line of demarcation. It is greatly to be hoped that this arrangement may not be confirmed ; for a river, so far from being a "natural boundary," must be, as a national highway, precisely a means of ensuring the existence of a more or less homogeneous population on either side of it. A river can hardly be a natural or national boundary except in time of war, and then one of the most unstable character. The only natural boundaries are evidently mountain-ranges and deserts; the only national boundaries are tribal frontiers which mark the termination of long-continued hostilities and the immediate establishment of national governments.

A. B. M.

(Namilonga)

(Moachimba)

Lekone or Lebaine

Moyana, 17°45'

(Mbupu's)
Mashotlana's
Sunjuia ferry
Victoria Falls

24° 26°

G. Philip & Son, London & Liverpool.

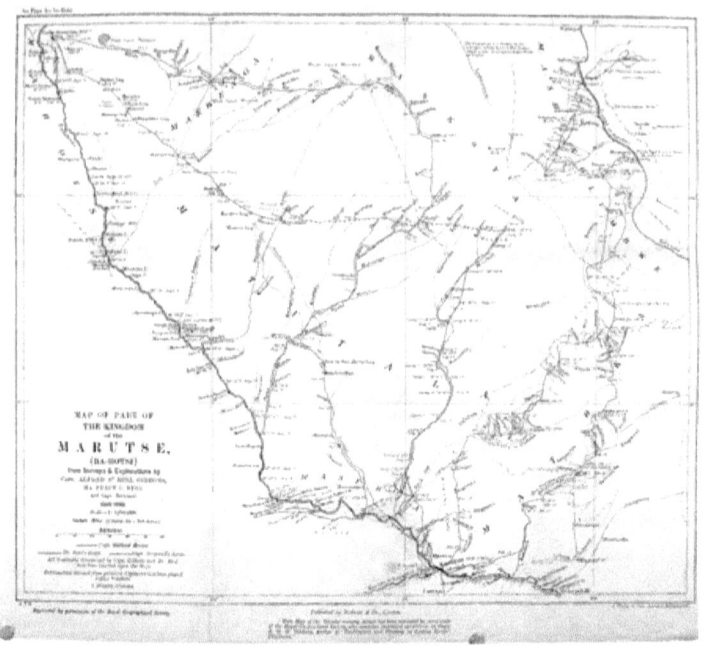

Échelle en milles anglais
0   50   100   150   200   250

Échelle Kilométrique
100   0   50   100   150   200   250   300 Kil

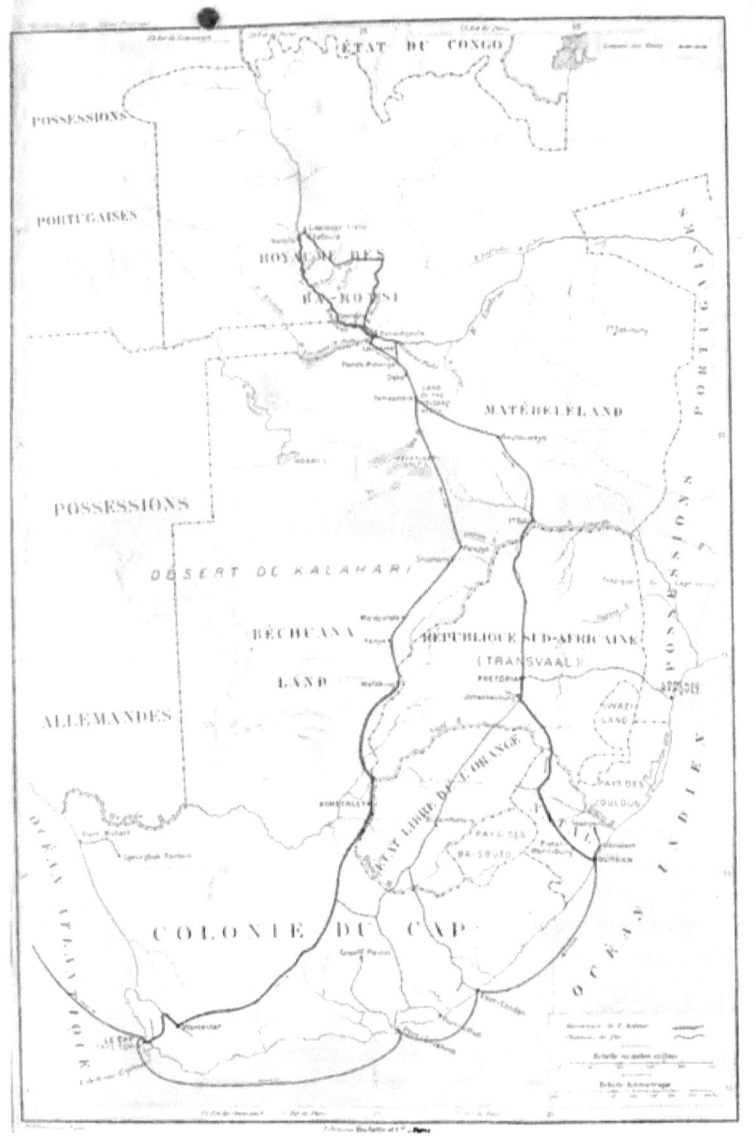

www.ingramcontent.com/pod-product-compliance
Lightning Source LLC
Chambersburg PA
CBHW030739230426
43667CB00007B/774